Strategic Pricing For Medical Technologies

A Practical Guide to Pricing Medical Devices and Diagnostics

CHRISTOPHER D. PROVINES

DEDICATION

This book is dedicated to my family Andrew, Christopher, Erin, and Dee.

CONTENTS

ACKNOWLEDGMENTS

I learned the hard way that writing a book is no simple endeavor. It takes time, energy, persistence, and a process. After twenty - plus years in the medical technology industry, with a lot of that time focused on pricing and value, I started down the path of writing this book so that I wouldn't forget what I've learned over the years.

Pricing is a complex area with many intricacies. I had an excellent marketing professor who said pricing and marketing is about "bringing the inside out, and the outside in." It's where the company's strategy, goals, innovation pipeline, and marketing and sales execution meet the customer and competitive realities. In this way, pricing is not a technical topic as some might make it, but really is a topic that requires a well-rounded business perspective.

I've had the good fortune to work in excellent businesses with some exceptional businesspeople who helped me develop my business perspectives. They say in sports that the hallmark of a great player is someone who makes those around him better. I've benefited personally over the years from working with many "great players" who made me better and supported my learning. These were bosses, mentors, colleagues, friends, as well as direct reports, far too numerous to list everyone.

In undertaking this project, a number of specific individuals provided support and insights. I would like to thank Paul Marshall of Marshall Healthcare Consulting for providing invaluable feedback on the reimbursement chapter. Paul is one of the top medical-devices reimbursement experts in the world and a genuinely nice guy. Mike Reiner, who is an expert in in-vitro diagnostics, provided many insights and ideas that helped shape the reimbursement chapter as well. Ravi Avva, a medical technology pricing expert, provided valuable comments, feedback, and ideas. Reed Holden, CEO of Holden Advisors, provided simple advice that proved profoundly beneficial in helping to complete this project. Lakshman Krishnamurthi generously volunteered his time and expertise in reviewing this text. I appreciate his kindness and valuable feedback.

From an encouragement and support perspective, many have pushed and encouraged me to write the book. I would be remiss if I didn't recognize special encouragement and support I received. I would like to thank the team at the Professional Pricing Society, Jason Aroesty, and Karl Schmidt. Finally, I wanted to thank my family for putting up with me camped out in my office writing.

PREFACE

Just imagine what our lives would be like without a robust medical technology industry. Over the past couple of decades, there have been significant advancements in the diagnosis, monitoring and treatment of patients. The medical technology industry has played a critical role in developing and commercializing many significant innovations. These range from drug-eluting stents to molecular diagnostics to better imaging modalities.

According to the industry association AdvaMed, rapid technology progress has resulted in a 15 percent decline in mortality from 1980 to 2000. The industry has an amazing array of innovations and services that have helped to improve and save the lives of a countless number of patients worldwide. In the hands of talented physicians and healthcare professionals, these tools and innovations have a profound impact on patient care. Most of us can think of specific instances in our own lives where family or friends have been positively impacted by this amazing industry.

However, today the medical technology industry sits at an interesting crossroads in its history. While the industry currently invests approximately 12 percent of its sales in research and development, its ability to capture the value of this investment is under serious pressure as governments, private payers, and providers around the world struggle with making choices on how best to fund all of this wonderful technology. Demographic trends, current healthcare spending levels, government debt crises, and other challenges are making this an even more difficult process for these key stakeholders.

Broadly speaking, the terms "med tech company" or "medical technology company" (as the terms are used in this book) are meant to capture all businesses that sell medical devices, medical supplies, diagnostics, and other goods and solutions that are used in the diagnosis, monitoring, and care delivery process in healthcare. This includes in-vitro diagnostics, in-vivo diagnostics, medical devices, medical supplies, implants, capital equipment, and services. This book is not intended to cover pharmaceuticals or biologics. These industries have their own unique pricing challenges.

From a pricing perspective, historically the industry has operated in a relatively easy environment. For many technologies, physician or user preference played a large role in product selection decisions, and economics played less of a role. Additionally, only in recent years have the payment systems in many parts of the world actively challenged the value of innovations. This meant med tech companies did not need to have a capability to understand value and set and manage prices strategically.

The world around med tech companies has changed and is continuing to change. Over the past few years, a number of drivers have emerged that have and will continue to challenge med tech companies like never before. These trends and drivers include: government debt crisis, demographic trends and the aging population, overall level of spending on healthcare, more sophisticated and demanding buyers, and the overall state of the economy.

These changes and trends will likely mean constraints in healthcare spending and lower reimbursement in many places. Thus, this will put pricing pressure on medical technology companies. Payers and health technology agencies have begun to challenge the clinical and economic value of new and existing innovations. These groups are looking for value for money and more intelligent ways to spend precious healthcare funds.

Finally, procurement or materials management as a profession has grown in its influence and impact in many industries. While healthcare is lagging behind, there is no doubt that the overall trends of professional buyers becoming smarter and more aggressive purchasers will greatly impact providers over the next decade. Value analysis committees in hospitals are now more widely used. This means hospitals and others involved in healthcare purchasing will put more pressure on med tech companies to prove their value as they become more savvy buyers.

Over the past two decades, the industry has responded to the increased role that economic buyers and payers have in product selection. The response has been to create or, in some cases, expand the reimbursement or payer function within the companies. Now, very few major companies are not without a reimbursement function. This is a necessary, but not sufficient, response to the challenges that face the industry. There is also a need in most companies to invest in understanding and communicating value as well as making smart strategic pricing decisions.

When I first became involved in pricing in the medical technology industry, it was about sixteen years ago. I began a process to become better educated about pricing strategies and tactics. Fortunately, there were some excellent general pricing books to learn from. *The Strategy and Tactics of Pricing*, by Reed Holden and Thomas Nagle, was an excellent reference at the time.

At that time, I also wanted to learn more about the specific issues in medical technology pricing. The closest book I could find was Mick Kolassa's book *Elements of Pharmaceutical Pricing*. This is an excellent book that deals with the pricing issues in the pharmaceutical industry. While certainly not a perfect fit for the medical technology industry, it has many concepts and approaches that I found useful for thinking about some pricing problems in medical technology.

So, why a book about strategic pricing for medical technologies? There are a number of excellent general pricing books available these days. Each has its strengths and weaknesses. In many cases, the principles and practices in these books can be applied to the medical technology industry. This is particularly true for the tactical elements of pricing. Whether a company sells a medical device, or a industrial good, or services in a business-to-business market, the tactical activities of managing discounts, preparing sales to negotiate better, defining price policies, or creating price analytics is shockingly similar across industries.

At the strategic level of pricing, many of the basic strategic pricing principles from other industries apply as well. This includes items like determining value, understanding demand, choosing a pricing strategy, and creating an offering strategy. However, it is the understanding of how to apply these principles to the unique industry context where the real difference occurs.

Over my twenty-plus-year career in the medical technology industry, I have always been struck by consultants with little med tech industry experience who would claim their general pricing expertise could be applied to the industry. I learned that 80 percent of the time, what they said was right. At a very high conceptual level, the basic strategic pricing principles and practices were fairly universal across industries. However, it was the other 20 percent, where the specific application of the principles to the industry or deep understanding of the industry context, that often made all the difference.

So, this book is intended to assist marketing, reimbursement, pricing, sales, finance, and others in the medical technology industry by filling in the other 20 percent. The intent is to provide frameworks, case studies, and insights to help apply strategic pricing principles to the medical technology industry and to better understand the industry context. The unique issues and challenges of the industry will be discussed, such as:

- How do you think about value for a medical technology?
- What inputs should you consider in developing a pricing strategy for a medical technology?
- Who are all the external stakeholders involved in a pricing decision, and how should you think about them?
- What roles does reimbursement play in the pricing decision?
- How should pricing and value be integrated into the innovation strategy?
- How do you integrate pricing and value into the product development process?
- What roles do clinical and economic evidence play in value communication and pricing strategy?
- How do you alter your offering to deal with different buyer types?
- How does contracting and pricing management differ for medical technologies?
- How do you manage international medical technology pricing?
- What ethical issues should you consider in setting prices?

My hope is that this book provides some new and helpful ways to look at strategic pricing for med tech companies. In the end, the fact that governments, payers, and hospitals are all becoming more savvy purchasers is a good thing. It will, hopefully, mean better spending of our scarce healthcare dollars. The days of companies launching new products with a few new features with uncertain value, and hoping for a price premium, are largely over. Unfortunately, for the unprepared company, the future could bring more pricing pressure, less market access, pressure on new innovations, and lower margins.

This book is not meant to provide the answers. Rather, it is an attempt to provide frameworks, tools, and the right questions. By asking the right questions, companies can think strategically about pricing and value. Hopefully, this will lead to better pricing decisions and help prepare med tech companies for a more challenging future environment.

PART I

INTRODUCTION AND CONTEXT

CHAPTER 1

WHAT MAKES MEDICAL TECHNOLOGY PRICING DIFFERENT?

Every industry has its pricing challenges. These challenges can be things like understanding buyer behavior, determining customer value, setting new product prices, or defining the right pricing strategy. Often, these challenges are similar across industries. Moreover, the approach to solving these challenges can often be similar across many business-to-business industries. This is because many of the basic fundamental principles of pricing and buyer-seller interaction apply to most industries.

At a high level, this is true for the medical technology industry as well. In many respects, the basic pricing principles that apply to other business-to-business markets would apply to the medical technology industry. Yet, the industry is different in many obvious and not-so-obvious ways when it comes to pricing. Obviously, the purpose of a medical technology makes the industry different. In the simplest sense, a medical technology exists to improve the quality of or to extend a person's life, or both. These goods are not consumed because people want them but are usually consumed to diagnose, monitor, or treat a human health issue.

The other obvious ways that the industry is different is the involvement of many different stakeholders and intermediaries in the product selection and buying process. Payers, physician societies, government agencies, and others play a role in influencing product selection and pricing. Even most other regulated industries lack the level of complexity and involvement of stakeholders that is present in the medical technology industry.

This chapter is meant to provide some framing and context for why the industry is different from a pricing perspective. With a clearer understanding of the industry context, strategic pricing decisions can be made. Without a clear understanding of the industry context, many mistakes will be made. These mistakes usually lead to poor sales and lower margins.

Pricing Medical Technologies vs. Industrial Goods

As an example, this may sound strange, but there are a lot of similarities in thinking about pricing for a steam-powered turbine that is used in a power plant and a computerized tomography scan (CT scanner). Steam-powered turbines are large capital equipment used to generate electricity in power plants. Manufacturers of these turbines sell the turbine as well as service and replacement parts. Often replacement parts and service can be a significant source of both revenue and profits.

A CT scanner is a piece of large capital equipment that is used in medical imaging procedures to produce a three-dimensional image of the inside of the body. Its purpose is to aid in the screening and diagnosis of disease and conditions (1). It is sold to hospitals and imaging centers. CT scanner manufacturers sell the capital equipment, service, spare parts, and software. Like with the steam turbines, parts and service can be a significant source of revenue and profits for CT scanner manufacturers.

The similarities do not end there. Both industries sell in markets where the demand is derived. That is, the demand for these products is derived by other upstream activities. Lowering the price of a steam turbine will not grow the overall market demand but rather could result in taking share from competing alternatives. Overall, market demand would be driven by electricity consumption.

In addition, both industries have to think carefully about the relative value that their offerings bring. The steam turbine and the CT scanner can address a wide variety of customer needs. This will often result in differences in the relative value the customer receives from the capital equipment, spare parts, and service. Understanding these differences across segments is critical for both industries.

As an example, a power plant that needs to run all of its turbines twenty-four hours a day, seven days a week, would need fast service response time when a turbine breaks down. However, a power plant with multiple backup turbines that can be used in case of an emergency would have a different service response time need. So, the customers with the differing operating needs would value service differently. The same analogy would hold true for CT scanner users. The operating situation and intensity of use would drive the customer needs and therefore the value the customer receives. Thus, in both cases, the manufacturers have to think clearly about the value of each of the components of their offerings.

Finally, industry regulation plays a big role in how the customers for the CT scanner and steam turbine manufacturers operate. Hospitals and imaging centers operate in highly regulated markets in most parts of the world. Insurers and regulators play a significant role in the usage of these technologies. Likewise, utility power plants tend to be highly regulated industries in many parts of the world. Regulation plays a part in how each industry operates.

Although there are many similarities in the two examples, a failure to understand the unique dynamics of the specific industry context can lead to many serious pricing mistakes. Therefore, getting pricing right for medical technology and services requires understanding how to apply pricing fundamentals and principles within the unique context of the industry. This is the focus of this book.

Why is Medical Technology Pricing Different?

This book will build on the basic fundamentals and principles of strategic pricing, including understanding value, defining a pricing strategy, developing an offering strategy, and communicating value. However, the focus will be on how to specifically apply these principles and practices to medical technologies. There are many unique complexities and dynamics of the medical technology industry that need to be considered in the application of strategic pricing, such as:

- *Patient care and access:* The purpose of a medical technology is to improve patient quality of life, to extend life, or to reduce the cost of care. Unlike a consumer good, people usually don't want to consume a medical technology. Consumption means there is a medical issue or problem that needs to be addressed. In addition, the pricing strategy selected for a given medical technology can impact whether patients get access to the technology. So, the medical technology company needs to carefully consider the ethical and policy issues in determining the right pricing strategy.

- *Value:* In the business-to-business context, many scholars and marketers have advocated focusing on the economic value of the offering in setting prices. Economic value is simply quantifying, in monetary terms, the difference between one offering and its next best alternative. While economic value holds true for medical technologies, it does not capture the entire value picture. Clinical value, that is improvements in quality of life and survival, play a significant role in the value equation. Therefore, medical technology companies have to consider the economic value and the clinical consequences when setting prices. There is also the issue of value from whose perspective. A medical technology may create significant value for a payer but little value for a hospital, as an example. So, from the perspective of value, one has to consider the multiple layers of stakeholders involved in purchase and use decisions.

- *Need to take a systems view:* Generally, in healthcare, medical technologies are inputs into the broader healthcare systems or care pathways. This simply means that the focus of pricing and value needs to move beyond the simple impact on one part of the system to looking at the broader system. For example, a manufacturer of a new blood test that can aid in faster diagnosis of ischemic stroke in the emergency room may only look at the benefits to one part of the care pathway, let's say the acute care hospital. However, a better test that improves diagnosis could have a profound impact on downstream costs in rehabilitation and assisted living.

- *Evidence:* Selling in any business-to-business context requires translating features and benefits into value for the customer. The same generally holds true for medical technologies. Yet, in the medical technology industry, the payers, users, and gate-keepers are usually looking for a very different level of evidence than in other industries. This is particularly true for new, innovative, and expensive technologies. Evidence in the context of medical technology means clinical and economic evidence of the cost and consequences of using the technology. This frequently requires an investment in gathering clinical and economic evidence. The type, quality, and depth of evidence can also drive the ability of the med tech company to justify the price it is charging.

- *Disconnect between user/chooser and who pays:* Depending on where in the world the med tech product is being used, there can be a disconnect between who uses the technology and who pays for the technology. Take the example of a US orthopedic surgeon who is in a private practice and performs surgeries at his local hospital. The surgeon is using and often choosing which medical technologies to use, but the hospital pays for the technologies. This can result in a significant disconnect. Hospital and payers have recognized this and have begun to implement a variety of mechanisms to try to align incentives (2).

- *Reimbursement and funding:* Private and government payers make decisions on whether to cover and pay for medical technologies or procedures. Payers and governments also decide on the level of healthcare funding in general. These reimbursement and funding decisions can have a significant impact on medical technology pricing. Therefore, understanding reimbursement and funding in the context of the pricing decision is crucial.

- *Stakeholders and public policy:* Pricing decisions often can be influenced by and have an impact on a variety of stakeholders, such as government policy makers, physician societies, and patient advocacy groups. Some serious pricing mistakes can be made by not understanding the influence and impact of these stakeholders.

- *Buying center:* The group of people in the customer account who make purchase and use decisions is called a buying center. These include the user, the chooser, and the gatekeeper (3). The nuances of how to assess the buying center and understand the relative influence of each member of the buying center often changes based on a number of factors. This can impact prices and demand. In provider organizations such as hospitals, the buying center dynamics can be very different from other industries. Understanding the unique differences is critical to smart pricing.

- *Buying groups:* In the US and other markets, different forms of buying groups have evolved to have a significant influence on pricing. These are large groups of customers who aggregate their purchases to negotiate better pricing and terms with manufacturers. Understanding how to evaluate and think about buying groups in the context of the pricing decision is critical.

- *Price and value referencing:* Since healthcare is publicly funded in many parts of the world, governments and others are often involved in the evaluation of medical technologies from a price and value-for-money perspective. This can result in transparency of prices and value assessments from country to country. In addition, in an effort to control healthcare costs, some countries are beginning to implement or consider price controls or price referencing systems for medical technologies. While this is already in place for pharmaceuticals, it is relatively new for medical technologies. Some medical technology companies, particularly those with high-cost technologies, will have to consider the potential and implications of price referencing.

There are many industry-specific factors that need to be considered in strategic pricing. The point of this list is not to over complicate pricing, but rather to highlight some specific issues that need to be considered in the pricing decision and to make the point that the industry context is important to understand.

Case Study: Home INR Testing

A real-life case will help illustrate some of the complexities of thinking about pricing and value in the context of the medical technology industry. Home INR testing is an excellent example for understanding the complexities of pricing, market development, and innovation in the medical technology industry. An entire new segment of the medical technology industry grew and expanded over the past decade to meet an unmet medical need. The technology was called home INR monitoring. INR stands for international normalized ratio, and it is a blood test used to measure the tendency of blood to coagulate (4).

The INR test can be used for a number of purposes. A large segment of users of the blood test is patients on a blood thinner called warfarin (5). There are a number of underlying conditions that warfarin is used to treat, including patients with mechanical heart valves and atrial fibrillation (AF). Warfarin is an old, inexpensive drug that is used to control the tendency of the blood to clot in certain types of patients. Warfarin was originally developed as a rat poison, but it was discovered to have beneficial effects in humans. However, warfarin has a narrow therapeutic window, which means there are safety issues and a wide number of possible side effects.

A large use of warfarin therapy is for patients who have atrial fibrillation (AF), or irregular heartbeat. AF is a condition that can lead to a stroke if it is not treated properly. In a patient with AF, blood pools in one of the chambers of the heart. The pooling blood can clot, and clots can travel to the brain and cause a stroke. Stroke is a devastating event for patients and their caregivers. It is also a very costly event for payers and society.

INR testing has been around since the 1980s. Traditionally, warfarin patients had to routinely travel to hospitals, physician offices, laboratories, or monitoring centers to have their INR levels tested. Warfarin is a dangerous drug since too much clotting can result in a stroke, and too little clotting can result in a serious bleeding event. While the warfarin is inexpensive, the cost of adverse events related to warfarin therapy is significant. Studies show that patients who have a bleeding event cost eleven thousand dollars in hospital costs per event (6). The cost of a stroke can be many multiples of that amount. Common medications and some foods also interact with warfarin, which makes it dangerous and causes the need for frequent monitoring.

One of the unmet needs and issues with INR testing was patient access to testing facilities. Some patients either do not have close access or are unable to get to a testing facility regularly. In addition, due to lack of convenience, some patients chose not to get tested regularly. This meant that patients risked having an adverse event due to lack of closely monitoring of INR levels.

Medical technology innovators tried to solve this unmet need by developing home INR testing technology. This technology follows the same basic idea of patient self-monitoring of blood glucose. It is now fairly routine for diabetic patients to perform self testing of blood glucose levels. There is also a business model and infrastructure in place to enable distribution and reimbursement of the diabetes testing devices and supplies.

In developing the technology, home INR manufacturers had to overcome a number of hurdles. It was not about simply developing the testing technology and setting a price. The companies had to develop the entire business model. A number of strategic choices and market drivers had implications for pricing. Equally important, choosing the right pricing strategy had the potential to impact the overall business model and adoption of the technology. The choices or drivers are as follows:

- *Value:* The home INR manufacturers had to understand the value of the new self testing idea across patient subsets to set the price of the new technology. Value was a critical input since, as is the case with many new medical technologies, value and price combine to form the cost of the therapy, diagnosis, or monitoring. Value was critical to convince payers to pay for the technology.

- *Evidence:* There was a significant concern, as there normally is, when patient monitoring goes from a central model to a distributed home monitoring. The manufacturers had to invest in evidence to prove that patients were able to conduct testing at home with a level of precision that is consistent with professional testing. This was a necessary input to unlock reimbursement.

- *Reimbursement:* At the start, the Centers for Medicare and Medicaid Services (CMS) only covered home INR testing for patients who had a mechanical heart valve. For AF patients, CMS did not cover and pay for patient self testing. Without any reimbursement mechanism, pricing was irrelevant. Since most patients tend to be older and have other medical conditions, without third-party reimbursement there would be little adoption of the technology regardless of the price.

- *Public policy and stakeholders:* The INR self-testing manufacturers had to be sensitive to the stakeholders and public policy issues involved. A movement to patient-based testing often means less revenue for those involved in the established diagnostic pathways. So, all things being equal, those in the established diagnostic pathway had no economic incentive to be big supporters of this testing. Other stakeholders involved included patient advocacy groups.

Ultimately, the INR self-testing manufacturers were successful in gaining expanded reimbursement coverage and funding for home INR testing for AF patients in 2008 (7). The devices were considered safe and a good value for money. Based on economic studies, the cost of home testing was slightly more than in-office testing. Studies showed that patient self testing was as accurate as in-office testing.

That is not the end of the story. By 2012, a number of pharmaceutical companies have launched or were poised to launch new classes of drugs that will replace warfarin for treatment of AF. Unfortunately for the home INR testing manufacturers, these new drugs will not require as frequent routine monitoring of INR levels. Many Wall Street analysts expect these new drugs to rapidly replace warfarin due to a better safety profile and the lack of a need to do as frequent INR monitoring. In fact, part of the economic value message for the new drugs is the ability to eliminate the costs related to frequent INR monitoring.

This story highlights some of the complexities of strategic pricing for medical technologies. It is not as simple as deciding on a pricing strategy based on the usual inputs that might be used for any business-to-business market. While those inputs should certainly be looked at, there are many other critical inputs to evaluate and decisions to be made. Reimbursement, investments in evidence, public policy, and a number of other unique aspects of the industry should be considered in pricing decisions.

Strategic Pricing Framework for Medical Technologies

Making the right strategic pricing decision can be a challenge. There are many factors to consider. Figure 1.1 provides an overview of the key elements of strategic pricing for a medical technology. In the inner circle are the critical elements of strategic pricing. This includes understanding customer value, defining a pricing strategy, developing an offering strategy, creating a contracting and tendering strategy, and, finally, communicating and selling value.

On the outside of the core strategic elements are critical inputs to and areas that influence the pricing strategy. These are the external environment, reimbursement and evidence, the buying center and buying groups, the innovation strategy, and international pricing. These are key areas where a lack of understanding can lead to the wrong pricing strategy or missed opportunities.

Figure 1.1 – Med Tech Strategic Pricing Framework

The remainder of the book is structured around this framework. Part I is an introduction and context setting. This includes a review of the external environment and public policy, and the implications for pricing. Part II addresses the core strategic pricing elements. This includes both a review of the strategy as well as a discussion of how to practically apply the thinking for medical technologies. Finally, Part III does a deep dive into the elements outside of the core pricing elements. These are critical areas to consider as part of strategic pricing. In fact, many of these areas are what separate the medical technology industry from other industries from a pricing perspective.

How to Use This Book and Some Caveats

In no respects should the reader misconstrue any of the content in this book as promoting pricing gouging, taking unfair advantage of the reimbursement system, or taking advantage of patients. The days of medical technology companies having poor pricing and value practices will come to an end. Governments, payers, and providers are becoming and will become much smarter purchasers of healthcare goods and services. In most parts of the world, there is simply no alternative. The healthcare spending trends, government debt levels, and other megatrends means the current approach to funding and procuring medical technology and services is unsustainable. The content in the book is meant to help medical technology companies get paid for a fair portion of the value that they create, and to be smarter about pricing and value decisions. This will hopefully help, perhaps in some small way, enable medical technology companies to be part of the solution to our collective healthcare challenges.

Conclusion

The basic pricing principles and fundamentals that apply to most industries also are applicable to the medical technology industry, principles like understanding value, pricing strategically, communicating and framing value, and managing pricing intelligently. However, there are a number of unique elements of the medical technology industry that need to be considered in pricing. Therefore, in order for medical technology companies to be successful at pricing, they have to both understand the fundamentals and know how to apply these to the specific industry context.

NOTES

1. Nordquist, C., (2009) "What is a CAT Scan?" MedicalNewsToday.com June 10, 2009. accessed June 28, 2012

2. Details can be found in 2010 Census Data. American Academy of Orthopaedic Surgeons. AAOS.org, accessed June 28, 2012

3. Bonoma, T., (2006) Major Sales: Who Really Does the Buying. Best of HBR July-August 2006

4. WebMD.com, accessed June 28, 2012

5. IBID

6. Kim, M. et al., (2010) Hospitalization costs associated with warfarin-related bleeding events among older community-dwelling adults. Pharmacoepidemiol Drug Saf. 2010 Jul;19(7):731-6

7. National Coverage Determination (NCD) for Home Prothrombin Time/ International Normalized Ratio (PT/INR) Monitoring for Anticoagulation Management. www.cms.gov, accessed June 28, 2012

CHAPTER 2

EXTERNAL ENVIRONMENT AND PUBLIC POLICY

The global market and external environment that medical technology firms operate in can be complex and confusing. One segment of the medical technology industry may have a different range of external factors influencing pricing than another segment of the industry. A lack of understanding of the external environment can lead to poor decisions in general and, specifically, poor pricing decisions.

A basic understanding of the market and external environment is a crucial step in many strategic pricing decisions. This chapter will provide an overview of the market and review key trends driving the need for better strategic pricing.

External Environment for Medical Technologies

Unlike other business-to-business industries, the medical technology industry is an industry with many external influencers of buying decisions. It is usually not as simple as selling a product to a single account. There are, in general, other entities and individuals involved in product selection and use decisions who need to be considered.

Take the example of a company selling a basic hospital supply like sutures to a hospital. In a case like this, there are likely to be multiple entities and individuals involved in the product selection decision both at the account level and outside of the customer account. These could include clinicians at the hospital, the hospital administration, group purchasing organizations who contract with the supplier, and distributors who distribute sutures to the hospital. Even in a basic supply item, there are numerous individuals and entities involved who influence purchase decisions.

On the other hand, consider the case of a company that sells a highly innovative new technology. The number of entities and individuals who influence product selection and use decisions could be significant. These could include physicians, hospital administrators, group purchasing organizations, private payers, and health technology assessment groups. If it is a highly controversial item, others like physician societies and patient advocacy groups could be involved. Thus, there are a number of individuals and entities who could affect and be affected by the pricing decision.

The environment med tech companies operate in can be visualized in the simplified model in Figure 2.1. Figure 2.1 provides a view of the flow of influence, reimbursement payments and rules, and goods and services. This is an important starting point for understanding the context of the pricing decision. The framework provides an overview of the key entities involved in purchase and use decisions.

As Figure 2.1 shows, there are thirteen stakeholder groups that need to be considered when setting and managing pricing for medical technology. These groups include payers (government or private payers), health technology assessment groups, utilization control companies, caregivers, providers, intermediaries, advocacy groups, and, last but not least, the patients.

Figure 2.1 – Medical Technology Stakeholder Ecosystem Map

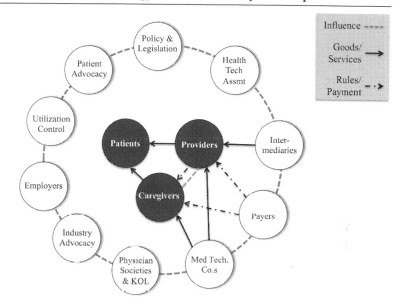

Obviously, depending on the type of product being sold and where value is created, these different groups may or may not play a role in pricing. For example, a company that sells surgical gloves may only need to be concerned with caregivers, providers, and intermediaries when making pricing decisions. On the other hand, a company that is launching a new innovative device to treat stroke patients may need to consider all of the groups when making a pricing decision.

While Figure 2.1 is a generalized view of the environment, it should hold true for most countries and product lines. However, there are still markets in the world where the patient pays directly for healthcare services or even acquires the medical technology or goods that will be used in his or her procedure.

At the center of the ecosystem are three groups. These are the patients, providers, and caregivers. Surrounding this core of the ecosystem are many different stakeholders who either provide goods and services or influence medical decisions. These stakeholders can have varying degrees of influence on medical decisions and product selection, depending on:

- Country's healthcare structure
- Reimbursement rules and policies
- Type of product or service being sold
- Product life cycle of the medical technology
- Relative amount of budget spent on the medical technology
- Perceived clinical and economic value of medical technology
- Degree of unmet medical need
- The clinician user
- The clinician specialty
- Relative influence of key opinion leaders

The next section will provide an overview and explanation of each of these stakeholder groups.

Key Stakeholders

Table 2.1, below, provides a more detailed explanation of each of the key groups along with some examples. In some cases, these groups play a very active role in evaluating the value and utilization of medical technologies.

Table 2.1 – Overview of Stakeholder Groups

Group	Explanation	Examples
Payers	Government payers and private insurers. These groups generally set the rules and payment levels for reimbursement of healthcare.	Private insurers such as Aetna, Center for Medicare and Medicaid Services, health ministry in many countries
Health Technology Assessment	Health technology assessment groups evaluate technologies and services for clinical and economic value.	UK's NICE, AHRQ, Canadian Agency for Drugs and Technologies in Health
Providers	These groups own the assets where healthcare services are provided and also provide the service of healthcare.	Hospitals, laboratories, radiology centers, outpatient surgery centers

Caregivers	The people and groups directly involved in the diagnosis and care of patients. Physician societies promulgate treatment guidelines.	Physicians, nurses, lab technicians, and physical therapists
Intermediaries	These groups include buying groups such as group purchasing organizations (GPOs). The group also includes distributors that physically move product.	Premier, Novation, Owens and Minor
Physician Societies	Physician organizations focused on scientific, educational, and advocacy efforts for its members.	European Society of Cardiology, American College of Surgeons
Industry Advocacy	Hospital, laboratory, and medical technology trade organizations that act on behalf of the association's members.	AdvaMed, American Hospital Association, Medical Imaging and Technology Alliance, European Diagnostic Manufacturers Association
Utilization Control	These are organizations that play a role in determining whether a medical technology or procedure is appropriately utilized.	Radiology benefits managers
Patient Advocacy	These are groups that promote research, education, and advocacy for specific disease areas or patient populations.	National Breast Cancer Coalition, American Diabetes Association
Employers	In many countries, employers provide access to and funding for health insurance. Employers can be influential in determining access to medical technologies for the employee population.	Large corporations

Pricing is a challenging decision, particularly for new important technologies. The medical technology company usually wants to ensure that it captures a fair portion of the value created by the technology and ensure a return on the investment to develop and bring a technology to market. The company also wants to ensure that patients who need the technology have access to it. Given that the price and utilization impact many different stakeholder groups, it is important to conduct an analysis to understand the implications.

Case study: Coronary Stents and JJIS

An example may help provide some perspective. In the 1990s, Johnson and Johnson Interventional Systems (JJIS), then a division of Johnson & Johnson (J&J), launched the palmaz-schatz stent. This was a new cardiac stent—a tint stainless steel tube that is mounted on a miniature balloon and is inserted into a patient's coronary artery during an angioplasty procedure. It was a technological innovation and was rapidly adopted by physicians.

At launch of this new technology, there was no incremental reimbursement provided to hospitals for the technology. JJIS launched the stent technology and charged $1,600 per stent. Since patients usually have 1.2 to 1.5 stents used per procedure on average to open clogged arteries; this meant the hospitals had to absorb $1,900 to $2,400 per procedure. This created a financial issue for many hospitals (1).

Making matters worse, JJIS refused to provide volume discounts for the technology. This meant that regardless of the number of stents purchased, hospitals had to pay the $1,600 per stent. The hospital industry buyers had become accustomed to volume-based discounting (2). So, the pricing strategy and tactics of JJIS flew in the face of this practice. Cardiologists accused JJIS of price gouging and began to urge the FDA to expedite approval of competitive products under review (3). J&J lost almost all of its stent market share once the competitive stents came to market.

From a stakeholder perspective, this story highlights a number of key issues that could have been considered prior to launch. First, without incremental reimbursement, most hospitals would have faced a significant adverse financial impact with the adoption of the technology. Second, interventional cardiologists faced significant pressure from the hospital administration. Next, the financial impact to the hospital varied by how many procedures it did. Hospitals that performed many procedures would be impacted much more than smaller hospitals that performed fewer procedures. Discounting the technology in the face of no reimbursement probably would have made sense.

For important new medical technologies, it is important to proactively think through the potential pricing implications for all of the stakeholder groups. As in the case with JJIS and the stent, proactively analyzing the impact on stakeholders may have had a different outcome. For each stakeholder, it is important to ask:

- How will the pricing strategy and tactics impact this stakeholder?
- What could be the implications of the pricing decision?
- Are there different tactics or actions that can be considered to mitigate any impact?

In the case of JJIS, a stakeholder analysis mapping exercise could have revealed a map like what is shown in Figure 2.2. The circles that are highlighted represent stakeholders that may have had an adverse or positive influence on the pricing decision.

Figure 2.2 –JJIS Case Example - Ecosystem Map

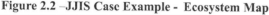

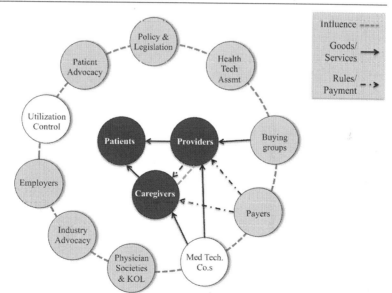

With a stakeholder analysis complete, the company could have moved on to thinking through how to mitigate any potential issues and also how to use stakeholders to positively influence outcomes. Obviously, the need to complete such a detailed analysis will depend on the size of the business opportunity and the relative risk that stakeholders can have on the pricing decision.

Public Policy and Medical Technology Pricing

Given that governments are the largest payers in many countries around the world, public policy can play a significant role in the utilization and price of medical technologies. Therefore, for expensive technologies, new technologies, or technologies that represent a relatively big-budget item, it is important to consider the policy implications of pricing decisions. At the end of the day, governments want to spend the limited healthcare funds wisely and get good value for money. If your pricing is perceived as not fair or not providing good value for money, there is significant risk.

Over the years, a number of governments have sought to directly intervene into pricing of medical technologies. In the US, for example, there is increasing noise about the cost of medical technologies. There is also a growing concern about price fairness and transparency. The Government Accountability Office (GAO) study released in January 2012 showed substantial variation in prices paid for implantable devices and concern that some hospitals are overpaying (4). The GAO went on to say that hospitals may not be getting the best prices possible and that the increased costs are passed on to the Medicare system and taxpayers (5).

The medical technology industry, through its industry association AdvaMed, tried to counter this assertion of unfair pricing and lack of price transparency by saying that the study only looked at a small set of devices, and it is not generalizable. In addition, the industry association points out that the government's own studies show that the price increases on medical technologies is below that of both broader medical price increases and general price increases in the economy as a whole (6).

In China, the government has sought to introduce rules and policies to strengthen control over medical device purchasing by state-owned facilities

(7). These rules create centralized purchasing for different types of medical technologies. Usually, expensive implantable devices are under the most scrutiny. In addition, the government has also sought to put price controls in the distribution chain to limit price increases and to control the amount of mark-ups that occur. All of these efforts by the government are to gain control of health expenditures and get good value for money.

In Europe, Canada, Australia, and other markets, price is controlled indirectly through a variety of mechanisms. These mechanisms include health technology assessments, reimbursement mechanisms, and sometimes specific price negotiations. As pressure increases on government budgets, there continues to be a growing push to use technology assessments to evaluate the necessity, effectiveness, cost-effectiveness, and feasibility of using medical technologies in various patient populations. There is formal and informal sharing of technology assessments across countries.

The sharing of health technology assessment evaluations across countries has widespread implications for pricing and utilization. A poor appraisal in one country could impact sales in another country. In addition, the prices that are included in one assessment can be shared with other countries. This means there is the risk of informal price referencing. The chapters on international pricing and reimbursement will address this topic in great detail. However, it should be clear that public policy can have significant potential impact on pricing and needs to be considered carefully.

Future of Medical Technology Pricing

As in any market, the role and influence of each of the market participants are not static. There are a number of trends and issues causing a shift in how healthcare decisions are made, which could influence pricing. These trends include accelerating healthcare costs, an aging population, government budget crisis, growing shortage of healthcare workers, and growing employment of physicians by providers in the US. These trends are likely to result in the following implications for medical technology pricing:

1. *Continued cost containment pressures:* Much greater emphasis on cost containment than in the past. This will impact both

pricing and utilization of medical technologies. Medical technology companies will need to think about pricing, product portfolios, and their offerings in the context of a cost-containment environment.

2. *Movement toward aligned incentives:* Increasingly, payers and providers are moving towards trying to align the financial interests of the providers and payers with the interests of the care providers. These include mechanisms such as gain sharing, where physicians are rewarded financially for controlling costs. In addition, in the US, there is a trend of physicians moving from self employment to being employed by providers. This will make aligning incentives easier and should give economic buyers more power in the buying decision.

3. *Rationing of new technologies:* Already in parts of the world, health technology assessment organizations make recommendations on which patient subsets should receive and not receive a therapy or procedure that involves a new medical technology. These recommendations are based on clinical as well as economic factors. This often results in products not being recommended for use in certain patient populations.

4. *Increasing need for economic evidence:* The growing focus on cost containment and economic value will mean that medical technology companies need to be skilled at understanding value, communicating value, and generating evidence to prove the economic value.

5. *Continued focus on evidence-based medicine:* Given the movement to cost containment and greater alignment between physicians and providers, higher priced technologies or alternatives will increasingly need some justification to support the pricing. Physician preference alone may not be enough to support a higher price or broad usage in the future. Beyond economic proof that a technology or supply is good value for money,

clinical evidence can play a role in helping to justify perceived higher price technologies or supplies. There has been a movement towards requiring greater evidence, and this will likely continue.

6. *Growing trend of buyers becoming more savvy:* Over the past decade, most businesses have invested in their procurement or purchasing functions. There is a long-term trend of organizations becoming smarter buyers of goods and services. While studies show that healthcare lags behind other industries, the ongoing cost pressures on providers makes it likely that they will become more sophisticated in their sourcing strategies and practices.

Conclusion

Strategic pricing of medical technologies will require a clear understanding of the external environment. Unlike other industries, the external environment for medial technologies is influenced by many stakeholders and market participants. These stakeholders and market participants can have an impact on pricing decisions. Equally important, there are a number of trends and issues driving the need for change in healthcare. These trends make it likely that economic buyers' power in buying decisions will increase over time. This will mean that medical technology companies need to think differently about pricing strategically, communicating value, and developing evidence. Unprepared companies will likely face significant pressure and poor results.

NOTES

1. Finkelstein, S., (2003) Why Smart Executives Fail. Penguin Group. New York, NY
2. IBID
3. IBID
4. Pecquet, J., (2012) GAO Report Spurs Call for Medical Device Price transparency. TheHill.com. February 6, 2012. accessed June 28, 2012
5. Report to the Chairman, Committee on Finance, U.S. Senate. Lack of Price Transparency May Hamper Hospitals' Ability to Be Prudent Purchasers of Implantable Medical Devices. January, 2012
6. Pecquet, J., (2012) GAO Report Spurs Call for Medical Device Price transparency. TheHill.com. February 6, 2012. accessed June 28, 2012
7. Lundy, S., et al. (2011) Before Entering the Chinese Medical Device Market, Know the Regulatory Landscape and Ready Your Resources. Medical Devices Law and Industry Report, 10/19/2011. http://www.bna.com

PART II

MEDICAL TECHNOLOGY STRATEGIC PRICING
FUNDAMENTALS

CHAPTER 3

UNDERSTANDING THE VALUE OF MEDICAL TECHNOLOGIES

What is value? In the medical technology industry, this can be a difficult question to answer. It often depends on the metric that is used to evaluate value. Is it clinical value, economic value, psychological value, or some combination of clinical and economic value? Also, this is often a question of perspective. A medical technology that provides value to a payer may not have the same perception of value by the hospital or provider.

What is clear is that value is something beyond just the features and benefits of the product or solution you are selling. Features are facts and data that describe the technology or offering. Value translates those features into economic and clinical terms. Yet, it is not unusual to see the key messaging and marketing collateral to be largely feature based and not value based.

This chapter takes a deep dive into value. The focus is on understanding and quantifying value from multiple stakeholder perspectives. Value is at the heart of pricing. It should be the key input to pricing strategy. Due to the growing cost pressures and funding issues for healthcare around the globe, value is also increasingly being used by payers and providers to evaluate medical technologies. So, it is critical that medical technology companies understand and can quantify their value.

Elements of Value: Clinical, Economic, Psychological

In order to get started, it is probably best to get grounded on what is meant by value. There are numerous definitions of value. In business-to-business markets, Anderson, Jain, and Chintagunta defined value as the worth in monetary terms of the economic, technical, service, and social benefits a customer firm receives in exchange for the price paid (1). In medical innovation, Cutler and McClellan define value as "the net change between the benefits and costs of the innovation (2). In their definition of value, there are two dimensions to benefits. The most important is the value of better health—longer life as well as improved quality of life. The second benefit is the effect on the financial situation of others. Another definition of value in medical innovation is the costs and consequences of one treatment compared with the costs and consequences of alternative treatments (3). Finally, Christensen defines value or value proposition as a product or service that helps customers do more effectively, conveniently, and affordably a job they've been trying to do (4).

As you can see, there are somewhat different definitions of value, but there are common themes. Value is usually quantifiable and is based on consequences or outcomes. Value includes the economic, clinical, and other benefits provided to stakeholders. Lastly, value is always relative to some alternative. Figure 3.1 provides an integrated way to think about value in the medical technology market. There are three key elements of value.

The first two elements of value, clinical and economic, tend to be more rational and quantifiable. These elements of value are also ones that payers, policy makers, and other economic buyers look to when making decisions. The third element of value is meant to capture all of the intangible elements of value involved in purchase decisions. Despite the need for quantitative value, individuals and groups making buying decisions are human beings. This means that decisions often involve subjective assessments of other non-quantifiable value.

The medical technology value pyramid is structured with clinical value as the foundation. On top of clinical value comes economic value. Finally, psychological value is on the top of the pyramid. While not always the case, this is one way to think about the relative priority of each of the three elements of value. When there is a high unmet clinical need and one technology performs much better than the next best alternative, than clinical value becomes the dominant form of value differentiation. When two technologies are similar in delivering clinical outcomes, then economic and psychological value become the basis of competition and value differentiation.

Figure 3.1 - Medical Technology Value Pyramid

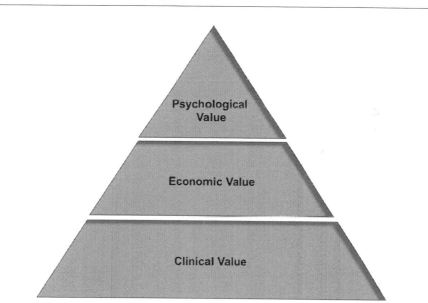

Clinical Value (CV)

The foundation of value in the medical technology market is clinical value. Meaningful differences in clinical outcomes matter. This assumes, of course, that there is evidence to substantiate the clinical differences. These clinical improvements are attributes such as better safety, effectiveness, improved diagnosis, meeting a previously unmet need, and quality-of-life improvements. Since the primary purpose of a medical technology is to improve human healthcare, this is the foundation of value for medical technologies.

Clinical value can be both anecdotal as well as evidence based. Anecdotal simply means that the caregivers can see the effects of the treatment or believe that the treatment or technology is having the intended benefits. Despite the movement to evidence-based medicine, much of clinical practice is still based on the perceptions and case history of individual clinicians. If the clinicians are able to directly observe the technology having an impact on patient outcomes, this is a powerful value element.

On the other hand, given the cost pressures in most countries around paying for healthcare, there is a significant movement towards evidence-based medicine. This is particularly true in markets where the government is the primary payer. The result is a need for medical technologies to prove clinical value through evidence. So, while a medical technology company may believe that its technology has significant clinical value, without evidence it will be difficult to substantiate value.

Economic Value (EV)

Economic value represents the quantifiable savings or benefits in monetary terms of one technology or service compared to an alternative. Economic value can be described and calculated in a variety of ways. There are also numerous metrics and quantification techniques that are used. These terms include total cost of ownership (TCO), budget impact modeling, and health economic metrics such as cost-effectiveness and cost-utility analysis. The topic of economic value will be explored in greater detail in this chapter.

Psychological Value (PV)

Psychological value includes things like brand, reputation, ease to do business, ease of use, and relationship. These benefits do not directly translate objectively into economic value, but depend on each buyer's subjective assessment of value (5). In business-to-business purchasing, the elements of risk and career consequences come together as an important driver of psychological benefits. The old saying "nobody ever got fired for buying IBM" is an example of this psychological benefit. Buying IBM was considered a safe bet and, therefore, had a psychological benefit. Psychological value, as is used in this framework, can include:

- Brand
- Risk
- Uncertainty
- Complexity
- Relationship and trust
- Convenience
- Ease of use
- Hassle factors
- Touch and feel
- Sales force knowledge and expertise

Take the example of two companies selling new surgical devices for a new surgical technique. Assume one company has a highly trained sales force that is perceived as expert in the technology, the surgical technique, and anatomy. Now assume the other company has a sales force that is perceived as much less competent in the all of the same dimensions. The company with the highly skilled sales force is, all things being equal, bringing greater value to the customer and should be able to command a price premium. As the new surgical technique matures, this sales force expertise may be less of a factor, but in the earlier stages of the market it is likely to be source of value.

Unlike the pharmaceutical market, many medical technologies are actual tools used by clinicians to treat and diagnose patients. This means that beyond a pure clinical and economic assessment of value, psychological elements can play a role in value. For example, a simple medical supply item like surgical gloves may seem like a commodity. However, a surgical glove that provides physicians much better dexterity could be highly preferred and have psychological value. It may be difficult to quantify the economic benefits of better dexterity, but the psychological benefits are certainly present.

Value from Whose Perspective?

One of the unique challenges of the medical technology industry is the fact that the same innovation may create widely divergent value for each of the stakeholders involved in healthcare delivery. For purposes of this discussion, stakeholders are defined as: patients, physicians/caregivers, payers, employers, and hospitals. The divergent value is often due to the complexity of the payment systems, the timing of changes to reimbursement, and other factors.

At times, an innovation can have negative value for one stakeholder group and significant positive value for others. For example, the first drug-eluting stents approved in the United States brought tremendous value to patients and payers. Yet, there was some indication that US hospitals initially tried to limit use due, in part, to the financial impact of the technology to the hospitals. While there was incremental reimbursement at launch of the technology, the reimbursement only considered the cost of care compared with a bare metal stent procedure. Hospitals feared that coronary artery bypass procedures (CABG) would be cannibalized by the technology. CABG is a very high-revenue procedure for hospitals (6).

The medical technology company will need to think carefully about where value is created in the healthcare value chain and who benefits. Part of this trick of assessing value is understanding the reimbursement system and incentives in the reimbursement system. Chapter eight on reimbursement provides a review of different reimbursement systems and mechanisms to help in understanding where value is created. This is why reimbursement is so critical to capture value in healthcare markets.

Payer Value Analysis

From a payer perspective, the basic assessment of value comes down to two key dimensions. First is the clinical impact of the technology or intervention. The other key driver is the financial implications or economics of the technology or intervention. This can be viewed in Figure 3.2, which shows a cost-effectiveness plane (7). On the vertical axis is clinical outcomes.

On the horizontal axis is costs or economics. In assessing a technology or intervention, the payer will need to decide:

- *Patient population*: What is the patient population that will be evaluated? It could be a very broad population or a relatively narrow population. For example, in evaluating a new wound-healing technology, the payer may look at all patients who have a surgical opening. On the other hand, a narrow patient population could be all patients who have a surgical opening and who are diabetic patients with a body mass index above thirty-five. In each case, the value of the technology and the economic impact to the payer's budget is likely to vary.

- *Comparator*: The technology or intervention needs to be compared to something to assess the value. The comparator could be to an alternative intervention, to drug therapy, or to doing nothing. As an example, companies are now launching percutaneous heart valve technology. This technology allows patients to have their heart valves replaced using a heart valve that is implanted using catheter-based technology. This minimally invasive surgery would be compared to medical management in patients who were too sick for open surgery, or it would be compared to open surgery.

- *Outcome*: How will clinical outcomes be measured? Will there be real clinical endpoints or surrogate endpoints? Real clinical endpoints would be direct measurable clinical benefits like overall survival, disease-free survival, less post-op care, and fewer repeat procedures. A surrogate endpoint is a measure of effect of a certain treatment that may correlate with a real clinical endpoint but doesn't necessarily have a guaranteed relationship (8).

In Figure 3.2, there are some clear positions of winners, losers, and some areas of uncertainty. For example, a technology that has better economics in terms of lower total costs and is better clinically is a clear winner. On the other hand, a technology that costs more and is clinically inferior is a clear loser. The other quadrants are less clear. A technology that costs more but provides improved clinical outcomes is an area of uncertainty. This is where the payer will need to assess the relative improvement in outcomes using a cost-effectiveness or cost-utility analysis, which will be discussed later. If the technology costs less but is less effective, this is another area of uncertainty.

Figure 3.2 – Payer Value Perspective

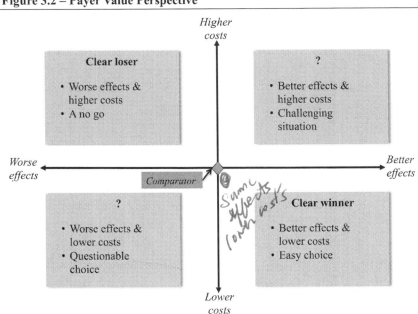

Value Analyses and Metric

There are a number of metrics and analyses that are used to evaluate whether a medical technology is good value for money from a payer perspective. We will discuss the primary ones here. The key point to keep in mind is that payers are often challenged with making choices about funding different technologies, procedures, or interventions. These often have some improvement to health, but can cost more. In order to evaluate whether a technology or intervention is good value for money, a number of metrics and analyses have been developed that bring together clinical value and economic value. Here is a summary of the key ones:

- *Budget impact modeling:* Budget impact modeling measures the net cumulative cost impact of an intervention, therapy, or diagnostic in a certain target patient population over a defined period of time. The analysis takes into account all relevant costs, both cost increases as well as cost offsets. It includes the costs for adverse events, the cost of the intervention, and all relevant follow-up costs within the scope of the system. The analysis looks at the overall system costs, such as for an entire hospital or managed-care plan. For example, a payer may want to understand the total budget impact of funding a new blood-based diagnostic test used for detecting early-stage colon cancer. In this analysis, the payer would look at the cost of paying for the screening test, the costs avoided by detecting cancer earlier, and the incremental costs that may result from false positives. The cumulative net costs would represent the budget impact. In this simple example, the payer could also look at the cost of providing the test to certain patient populations such as higher risk patients with a family history of disease. These budget impact modeling insights could be used to make reimbursement and coverage decisions. For medical technology companies that sell products with a potential system-wide impact, it would be important to understand the potential impact using budget impact modeling.

- *Cost-effectiveness analysis:* Cost effectiveness is a form of analysis used to evaluate health programs, treatments, and technologies. This analysis takes into account both the cost and health consequences of the treatment (9). The metric is usually based on a payer or societal viewpoint. The health consequences or effectiveness is usually measured in one single type of objective. Examples would be years of life gained for a implantable device, repeat procedures avoided for a new surgical intervention, cases detected for a diagnostic screening technology. The measure of effectiveness can be a final health output such as life-years gained, or it can be an intermediate output such as cases found (10). As an example, researchers conducted cost-effectiveness analyses of drug-eluting stents. Drug-eluting stents are tiny metal scaffolds coated with a drug that elutes over time. The stents are used to prop open coronary arteries following a balloon angioplasty. The health output used in this technology was repeat revascularizations avoided. Thus, researchers were able to measure the cost per repeat revascularization avoided for drug-eluting stent procedures. With this in hand, the cost of drug-eluting stent procedures could be compared to other treatments and interventions used to treat coronary artery disease such as non-drug-eluting stents and coronary artery bypass procedures. The important point about cost-effectiveness analysis is that it uses a common metric of health consequences for a given clinical field. It does not work as well when comparing a treatment in one clinical field to another where the underlying health consequences are different.

- *Cost-utility analysis:* Cost-utility analysis is a form of health economic analysis that measures the quality of the health outcome delivered by a treatment or diagnostic relative to the cost (11). Cost-utility analysis differs from cost-effectiveness in that the measure of health outcomes or effects is a common utility that can be used across clinical fields. Therefore, a payer could compare the utility of a new treatment for aortic valve disease with a new technology for diagnosing liver disease. In this case, the utility is usually expressed as quality-adjusted life-years (QALY). Typically, the incremental cost of a treatment or diagnostic is compared to the incremental health improvement measured in QALYs gained. QALY gained measures improvements in patient survival that are adjusted for quality of life. The result is usually expressed as cost per QALY gained (12). This metric is used by a number of researchers, health technology assessment organizations, and payers in making decisions about funding new technologies or treatments. The cost-utility analysis is also used to evaluate existing treatments and procedures to determine if they are a good value for money.

Case Study: ICDs in Canada

An example might help illustrate some of the concepts discussed in this section. Implantable cardioverter defibrillator (ICD) is a costly device for patients at high risk of sudden cardiac death. Heart disease may be complicated at any moment by a sudden, unexpected, and fatal abnormality of heart rhythm. A disorganized, chaotic rhythm termed "ventricular fibrillation" (VF) can occur. A person who develops VF has no effective circulation of blood to the body, which leads to brain damage within minutes and death shortly thereafter (13).

The cost effectiveness of ICDs were compared to drug-therapy in the Canadian Implantable Defibrillator Study (CIDS). The study showed that over a 6.3 year period, patients receiving ICDs had a higher life expectancy of 4.58 years on average compared with a life expectancy of 4.35 years for drug therapy. The question then becomes what is the cost to provide this health benefit. In this study, the cost of ICD therapy was C$87,715 per patient versus the cost of drug-therapy of C$38,800 per patient over the study period. Therefore, the study showed that it costs a little over C$49,000 (C$87,715 less C$38,800) to gain 0.23 additional years of life expectancy. The incremental cost-effectiveness of ICD therapy versus drug therapy was roughly C$213,000 per life year gained (C$49,000 divided by 0.23 years gained) (14).

As was mentioned previously, medical technologies often have a different effect or benefit across patient populations. In the case of ICDs, the CIDS study showed this to be true as well. Analysis showed that three risk factors were associated with better ICD benefits. When the cost-effectiveness analysis was computed for patients who had two or more of these risk factors, it showed that ICDs had an incremental cost-effectiveness ratio of C$65,195 per life year gained. Patients with fewer than two risk factors had a incremental cost-effectiveness of ratio of C$916,659 per life year gained (15). It

41

is clear from this example that understanding the value of the technology across different patient populations could possibly lead to different targeting and commercial strategies for the medical technology company and different reimbursement and funding decisions for the payers.

Implications for Value and Pricing

From a pricing and value perspective, the question of what is an acceptable amount to pay for incremental health effects or benefits such as life years gained is a controversial one. It differs across countries and there is often uncertainty around this amount within a country (16). It is generally thought that the willingness to pay for one quality adjusted life year (QALY) gained is between $50,000 and $100,000 in the United States. Researchers studied willingness to pay across countries and found that across the US, UK, Australia, and Japan, the willingness to pay for one QALY gained in US dollars was between $36,000 and $65,000 (17). As you can see, there is a wide range. From a pricing perspective, the medical technology company should be trying to answer a couple of simple questions:

- At what price is the technology cost-effective for a given country and patient population?
- Does the cost-effectiveness vary across different comparators?
- How does cost-effectiveness vary across patient subgroups?
- At a cost-effective price for the payer, what are the implications for the provider's economics and business model?
- Based on the cost-effectiveness for the payer and the provider economics, what is the pricing implications for the technology?

Case Study: CT Colonography in USA

The case of CT colonography provides a nice example of the connection between payer cost-effectiveness analysis, provider economics, and pricing. As part of a national coverage decision for Medicare in the USA, researchers reviewed CT colonography as a tool for colorectal cancer (CRC) screening in the Medicare population. CT colonography, which is often referred to as "virtual colonoscopy", was compared with a number of other CRC screening strategies including colonoscopy and fecal immunochemical tests. In the analysis by the Agency for Healthcare Research and Quality (AHRQ), researchers found that at a charge to the payer of between $100 and $230, that virtual colonoscopy would be a cost-effective screening strategy. This would be the cost to the payer, which includes the provider and physician fees. At the time of the study, charges for similar CT scan procedures in other application such as the abdomen were roughly $500 per procedure for the provider portion of the fee only. The very low cost-effectiveness values for virtual colonoscopy likely meant that the provider economics did not make sense. A total payment of between $100 and $230 for virtual colonoscopy would have left no economic benefit to the provider. Ultimately, the Centers for Medicare and Medicaid Services (CMS) decided that there was not enough evidence to cover CT colonography in the Medicare population (18).

In the analysis above, researchers not only reviewed the cost-effectiveness of the technology, but also tried to determine the fee to the payer at which the technology or services would be cost-effective. With these insights, the medical technology company can conduct modeling of the provider's economics and business model to determine the potential price of the technology to the provider. The medical technology company can then try to understand its own economics and whether the price to the provider would make good business sense. In a situation like this, where there is no established reimbursement for the service or technology, the value and pricing assessment starts with the payer's perspective and works backwards.

Study and Modeling Design

If you have a technology that lacks reimbursement or has inadequate reimbursement, this will often require working with payers to influence them to pay more for the technology or intervention. This will usually require studies and/or some form of modeling to prove the clinical and economic value. From a pricing and value perspective, these studies and models should:

- Meet acceptable standards – the studies and modeling should follow established guidelines for research practices for cost-effectiveness and decision-analytical modeling.
- Answer key questions – the studies should be designed to anticipate and answer the payers' key questions. This will often include clinical and economic endpoints, data requirements, subgroup analysis, sensitivity analysis, and modeling of uncertainties.
- Be designed with input – companies should get payer input prior to the design of a study or beginning any extensive analytic modeling. The input should include feedback on the comparators, subgroups, data elements, methodology, and other needs of the payers.
- Build awareness and influence – the studies and modeling should be designed and presented in a way to help build awareness and influence change. The studies and modeling should help highlight the clinical and economic burden of the disease or condition, the unmet clinical needs, and disease management implications for payers. Ultimately, these studies should be part of a broader publication strategy.

An in-depth review of the mechanics of the last two analyses and study design is beyond the scope of this book. The point of reviewing the metrics and analyses is to provide some perspective of how different payer stakeholders will evaluate value. Since the development and management of these studies is beyond the scope of this discussion and is, fortunately, already captured in some excellent texts (19), the focus for the remainder of this chapter will be on economic value and budget impact analysis. In the end, this is probably what many stakeholders, from hospitals to payers to intermediaries, want to understand. Even payers who evaluate technologies using cost-effectiveness or cost-utility analyses will also want to understand the budget impact.

Provider Value Analysis

A provider is a hospital, surgical center, laboratory, or other entity that owns the assets where care is delivered. It is important to understand value from this stakeholder's perspective. From the provider perspective, the basic assessment of value also comes down to two key dimensions—clinical outcomes and financial impact. This is not to say that product differences such as ease of use, convenience, and other factors do not matter. The assumption is that many of those differences can be quantified and translated into financial impact.

Financial impact is used since it is broader than costs or total costs of ownership. Total cost of ownership is a common term and means the cost to acquire, operate, maintain, and dispose of a solution. Financial impact is meant to capture the total financial impact of using a technology or intervention, which includes reimbursement. This means it captures both costs and revenues.

Figure 3.3 provides a simple provider value comparison matrix (20). This is a visual way of understanding how a provider might think about comparing one supplier's solution to another or one treatment method to another. On the vertical axis is clinical outcomes, and the horizontal axis is financial impact. As in the payer framework, a technology that provides better clinical outcomes and an improved financial impact is better for the provider and is usually a winner. Likewise, a technology that has worse financial outcomes for the provider and worse clinical outcomes for the patient is usually a loser.

The other positions on the matrix are either less clear or less dominant positions. Positions three and four should be winners. This is where the product or solution is the same in one dimension but better in another dimension. Similarly, positions five and six should be relatively clear as well. This is where the product is the same in one dimension but worse in another dimension.

Positions seven and eight are questionable. This is where the solution is worse than the alternative in one dimension, but better in the other dimension. Many new technologies in healthcare end up in position seven. This is where the technology provides better patient outcomes than the alternatives, but is worse for the provider from a financial perspective.

In the past, many providers knowingly accepted that new technologies start out in position seven. They were willing to accept the adverse financial impact in the hopes of being on the cutting edge, building a new clinical service line, or feeling as though there is no alternative given the clinical benefits of the technology. With the growing financial pressure on providers, this is becoming more difficult for them to handle.

Position eight is where the technology is better financially but worse clinically than the alternative. When markets mature, technology often becomes seen as "good enough." While a particular technology may be seen as somewhat inferior to an alternative, it may be deemed good enough. With a better financial impact to the provider, it could be a winner.

Finally, position number nine is where the technology is roughly the same clinically and financially to the provider. In this position, the dominant form of differentiation might then move to some other basis of competition. These could be things like the psychological value elements mentioned, such as brand, reputation, relationships, or other factors.

Figure 3.3 – Med Tech Provider Value Matrix

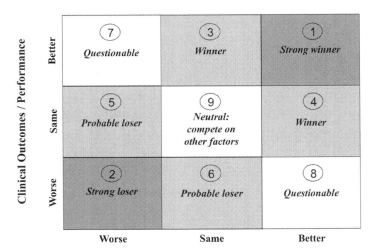

Financial Impact / Efficiency

An added area of uncertainty is when the comparison happens across clinical departments in a provider organization. For example, consider a new minimally invasive technology that is used to treat brain aneurisms in the catheterization lab. This procedure could be better in both financial impact as well as clinical outcomes for a select patient population.

However, if the technology is replacing a procedure that is done in the operating room by a different physician specialty, then the comparison of economics and outcomes becomes more difficult. Since the different departments are controlled by different specialties, there is the possibility that the value comparison is not as straightforward. This is when the medical technology company needs to work at a different level in the customer organization to make the value comparison clear.

Conduct an Initial Value Assessment

It is important to understand that each differentiated benefit of a product or offering could impact multiple elements of value. For example, a new antimicrobial suture that reduces the rate of infection in certain procedures has the potential to impact all elements of value. Reducing infection rates could improve clinical outcomes, could result in lower overall costs due to the use of fewer drugs to treat infections, and could provide psychological value to the surgeons. The initial value assessment helps to give a big picture perspective of potential sources of value prior to trying to quantify the value.

Table 3.1 provides a list of potential sources of value in the medical technology marketplace. The most promising potential benefits are those that create all three types of value—clinical, economic, and psychological. The individual benefits that are able to impact all three dimensions tend to be clinical in nature. However, they do not have to be restricted to clinical only.

For example, a new medical device that is significantly easier to use and reduces cycle time of a surgical procedure may be initially viewed as a source of economic value. Because it reduces surgical time, the manufacturer could promote the value of improved operating room capacity and scheduling flexibility. However, it is often helpful to dig a little deeper. The ease of use of the device could also translate into better clinical outcomes since the surgeon may not need to work as hard to achieve a successful surgical outcome. It could also impact psychological value since physicians will benefit from the ease of use. Therefore, something as simple as reducing surgical time could have multiple benefits.

Table 3.1: Initial Value Assessment Checklist

Value element	Potential sources of value	Why it matters
Clinical	Better safety	Improvement in mortality rate
Clinical	Improved effectiveness	Fewer repeat procedures or tests, improved patient quality of life, lower length of stay, less downstream costs
Clinical	Unmet needs	Address area of unmet clinical need
Clinical	Ease of use	Reduce time to learn and use, potentially better clinical outcomes
Economic	Maintenance	Reduces non-value-added time spent maintaining equipment or product
Economic	Training quality, requirements	Reduce training needed to educate users on operating the technology or using the device
Economic	Operating labor required	Fewer resources needed to operate the equipment or prepare the devices and supplies
Economic	Worker retention	The costs avoided in hiring and training new workers
Economic	Worker safety	Reduce lost work days or other costs related to healthcare workers' workplace safety events
Economic	Service needs	More robust reliability of equipment means fewer service visits, fewer spare parts, and less downtime
Economic	Cycle time	Solution reduces customer cycle time to complete procedure or diagnostic
Economic	Knowledgeable sales force	Sales force helps educate customer on solutions and technology
Economic	Inventory management	Able to reduce customers' inventory costs
Economic	Better service	Faster response, higher quality service technicians, and more knowledgeable customer service lowers customer costs or improves uptime
Economic	Ordering and shipping	Less time and effort required in ordering and receiving
Economic	Access to supplier capabilities	Able to take advantage of supplier capabilities to improve customer business
Economic	Acquire and disposal	Lower costs to acquire and dispose of supply or technology

Economic	Revenue	Able to help customers grow revenue through increased capacity or attract new patients
Psychological	Brand	Trust and belief in supplier
Psychological	Touch and feel	Improve clinician dexterity
Psychological	Convenience	Improve overall experience with company as a supplier
Psychological	Relationship	Experience with company and its representatives
Psychological	Employee engagement	Improve overall healthcare worker employee engagement
Psychological	Key opinion leader support	Helps provide credibility to the medical technology as a solution
Psychological	Quality of clinical evidence	Particularly for new or controversial technologies, the level of clinical evidence is critical in supporting value

Case Study: Safety Needles

Accidental needle sticks from conventional needles can be a significant safety issue for healthcare workers. Healthcare workers in the US suffer an estimated 600,000 to 800,000 needle sticks per year. With a host of blood-borne pathogens such as HIV and hepatitis potentially in the dirty needles, hospitals and other healthcare facilities face significant potential costs related to needle sticks. It is estimated that each needle stick costs $3,000 alone in testing and monitoring to determine if the injured worker has become exposed to a dangerous pathogen (21).

Given the significant safety issues, new devices called safety or retractable needles were developed. Immediately after use, these devices retract the needle back into the device to protect workers from needle sticks. In addition to avoiding needle sticks, the technology also enables lower disposal costs since the retracted needles take much less room in disposal containers (22).

A quick review of safety needles as compared with standard needles leads to the initial value assessment below. There are five key areas of potential value identified. Four of the five elements of value are related to economic value and should be easy to quantify. The fifth area relates to psychological value and, while harder to quantify, has significant potential leverage.

Table 3.2: Safety Needle Value Assessment

Value element	Potential sources of value	Why it matters
Economic	Training quality, requirements	Reduce training needed to educate healthcare workers on how to handle unsafe needles
Economic	Worker retention	The costs avoided in hiring and training new workers due to fear of being injured
Economic	Worker safety	Reduce lost work days or other costs related to health-care workers workplace safety events
Economic	Acquire and disposal	Lower costs to dispose of supply or technology
Psychological	Employee engagement	Improve overall healthcare worker employee engagement

Calculating Economic Value to Provider/Payer

In evaluating medical technology value, there are a number of analytical approaches to estimating value. Estimating value usually requires quantifying the economic impact of the technology. Choosing the right approach to estimating value comes down to understanding what value is created, who value is created for, and how value will be assessed. There are five steps to estimating value:

(1) *Define* potential differentiated benefits: Compare the technology or service to the next best alternatives to determine potential sources of value creation.

(2) *Identify* who benefits: Identify which of the stakeholders involved will benefit or receive value from the technology.

(3) *Select* correct value metric: Different stakeholders have differing ways to assess value. Select the right metric or analysis for the stakeholder.

(4) *Measure and quantify*: Measure and analyze the economic and clinical value created for each stakeholder.

(5) *Confirm and validate*: Confirm value assessment and validate through communication or guarantees.

Step 1: Define potential differentiated benefits.

This step involves assessing the potential differentiated benefits of the technology or solution. What does it do? How is it different than other available alternatives? For example, let us use the hypothetical case of a near-patient rapid blood test that could be used in emergency rooms to accurately diagnose someone having an ischemic stroke. Ischemic stroke is caused by a blood clot that blocks or plugs a blood vessel in the brain. About 80 percent of strokes are ischemic (23).

Despite all of the medical advances, stroke is poorly diagnosed and treated today in most countries. Patients with ischemic stroke, even with relatively mild symptoms, may be eligible for intravenous thrombolysis or other means of reperfusion if treatment can be started within a few hours of symptom onset. The challenge is often access to the right technologies and the speed to properly diagnose ischemic stroke. Computerized tomography (CT) is often normal after the onset of ischemia and may remain normal in patients with mild ischemic strokes (24).

So, what would be the benefits of a near-patient technology that successfully diagnoses ischemic stroke? While in a case like this, it may be appropriate to map the current diagnosis and treatment process, at a high level, there should be a number of significant potential benefits.

1) Better patient outcomes (quality of life, mortality)
2) Reduced treatment cost
3) Reduced rehab and follow-up costs
4) Replace expensive imaging technologies

Of course the benefits will really depend on the performance of the technology. Will the test be able to replace imaging technologies or be used alongside imaging? Will the test be able to distinguish between ischemic and the other form of stroke—hemorrhagic? What kind of clinical expertise is required to run and interpret the test? How sensitive is the test? Will clinicians use results of the test and change clinical practice? There are many open questions about the value, but at this point you should have a clear idea of the potential benefits.

Step 2: Identify who benefits.

Based on an analysis of the benefits of the technology, it should be fairly easy to identify who actually benefits from it. In this hypothetical case, there are a number of stakeholders who would benefit from such a technology. Table 3.3 provides a summary of the stakeholders and the potential benefits.

Table 3.3: Stakeholder Benefits Summary

Stakeholder	Benefits
Patient	Improve outcomes (quality of life, survival)
Payers	Improved patient care, reduce costs
Hospitals	Potentially reduce treatment costs, potentially reduce other diagnostic costs, better patient care
Physicians	Improve patient care

Step 3: Select the correct value metric or analysis.

For each of the stakeholders, it is important to identify the right value metric. This simply means understanding from their perspective how the value will be assessed. Depending on the viewpoint, there could be different ways for assessing and understanding value. For example, certain reimbursement authorities or health technology assessment groups may look at cost per quality-adjusted life-year gained (cost per QALY gained) as a metric. On the other hand, the hospital that purchases the new technology may be concerned with the financial or budget impact of the technology. Table 3.4 provides some examples:

Table 3.4: Examples of Value Metrics

Example Technology/Solution	Whose point of view?	How might value be measured?
Diagnostic test to accurately predict colon cancer patients' likelihood of needing chemotherapy	Payer	Budget impact analysis or cost-effectiveness analysis
Neurostimulation device that works to minimize the damage that results when brain cells are deprived of oxygen and nutrients	Payer	Cost-effectiveness analysis
New cardiac arrhythmias ablation technology that speeds up procedure	Hospital	Economic value to customer

At this point, if there is uncertainty on how these stakeholders will assess value, it is important to do basic primary research to ask the question. For example, if there is debate on how payers might think about and assess a given technology, it is important to ask them. This can be accomplished through some simple primary research techniques.

Step 4: Measure and quantify value.

With steps 1 through 3 complete, you should have a good idea of the potential benefits, who value is created for, and how the stakeholders will evaluate value. Next comes measuring and quantifying the value. This involves studying how the solution impacts the economics of each stakeholder and overall clinical outcomes. A few examples might illustrate how this works.

Case Study: Drug-eluting Stents—Payer Budget Impact Analysis

Let's use drug-eluting stents as an example. Bare metal cardiac stents are tiny metal scaffolds that are inserted into a cardiac artery via a catheter that is usually inserted in the femoral artery. The problem with bare metal stents is that some portion of patients' arteries re-clog some time after insertion of the bare metal stent. A new technology called drug-eluting stents (DES) was developed. The DES were essentially bare metal stents coated with a drug that elutes over time and reduces the number of patients having a re-clog of the same area and a needed repeat procedure.

Taking a payer perspective and evaluating DES from a budget impact standpoint will help illustrate the example. For bare metal stent patients, roughly twenty-eight in every one hundred patients would need a repeat procedure or repeat revascularization. For DES patients, roughly thirteen in every one hundred patients would need to have a repeat revascularization. Therefore, for every one hundred patients treated with a DES, the payer would avoid paying for fifteen repeat procedures. Assuming the treatment and follow-up costs for a repeat revascularization are roughly $16,500 each, the value created, not including the incremental costs of DES, to the payer would be $247,500 for each one hundred patients or $2,475 per patient (25). Assuming similar outcomes in terms of mortality and quality of life, then the DES should have an incremental value of $2,475 per patient from a payer perspective.

The incremental value for DES is the average per patient. Since coronary stenting procedures involve multiple stent implants per procedure, the incremental value of the DES per stent would be different. Using an average number of implants of 1.4, this means the incremental value per stent would be $2,475/1.4, or approximately $1,800 incremental per stent.

While this is a simplified example of a budget impact analysis, it does help illustrate the case for some simply messaging related to value. In this case, treating one hundred patients with the new technology would mean that payers would avoid paying for fifteen repeat procedures. In many cases, health outcome and economic studies will need to be completed to complement the simple messaging.

Case Study: Diagnostic for Breast Cancer—Payer Budget Impact Analysis

Take the example of Genomics Health (GHDX). GHDX is a California-based innovative diagnostics company. Oncotype DX breast cancer assay is a multigene expression test, developed and marketed by GHDX. The test is used by physicians to predict the likelihood of chemotherapy benefit and recurrence risk for patients with early-stage, estrogen-receptor-positive breast cancer. Prior to this test being available, doctors relied on treatment guidelines that took into account inputs like the size and type of cancer tumor, to decide who should receive chemotherapy.

From a payer perspective, the payer may be interested in the cost-effectiveness and the budget impact of the new diagnostic. For purposes of this discussion, the focus will be budget impact. A study of the economic impact of using the GHDX test to direct treatment provides some insights on value from a payer perspective. The study showed that the test had two main benefits. Out of one hundred patients, the test predicted that two previously categorized low-risk patients would be classified as intermediate/high risk. Also, the test predicated that forty-five previously categorized high-risk patients would be categorized as low risk. Use of the test in one hundred patients will cost $345,000 since the company had set the price in the US at $3,450 per test. The study showed that the cost of adjuvant chemotherapy will decrease by 46 percent, from $1.63 million to $876,000. Overall costs were projected on average to decline by 5 percent, from $4.32 million to $4.12 million, for a net savings of $202,828 (26). Therefore, the technology had a positive impact on the budget of the payer.

Case Study: Patient Ventilator—Economic or Financial Value to Customer Analysis for Hospital

Ventilators are machines that pump oxygen into sick patients' lungs. They cost between $3,000 for basic models to $40,000 for sophisticated models. Like many purchases, especially equipment purchases, it is important to look at not just the acquisition cost but also the total cost of the various solutions. Total cost of ownership (TCO), as the term is used in purchasing, means quantifying differences in the short- and long-term impact of not just the direct purchase price, but also all the costs and benefits associated with acquiring and using alternative offerings. For marketers, this should sound very similar to value, or economic value to customers, or customer financial impact.

When comparing alternative offerings, there are many potential costs or benefits to consider. These could be in areas like delivery, setup, maintenance, defect rates, rework, effectiveness, ongoing operating costs, and training. In fact, one cross-industry survey of procurement managers identified thirteen potential categories and 237 individual cost drivers where there could be meaningful differences (27).

Many of the categories and type of value or total cost of ownership examples from the cross-industry study hold true for healthcare. In addition, there are a number of other ones to consider for healthcare. For example, in hospitals with very high occupancy rates, reducing length of stay can have a big financial impact. This is because hospitals are often paid a single payment per patient called a DRG (diagnosis-related group) in many countries. Often the payment is the same regardless of the length of stay. Therefore, if hospitals can reduce length of stay while maintaining the same quality of care, they can improve asset utilization and profits. Table 3.5 provides a list of categories and examples of potential total cost of ownership differences.

Table 3.5: Categories of Potential Value or TCO Differences

Category	Example(s)
Operating cost	Efficiency, capacity
Quality	Rework, inspection
Logistics	On-time delivery, availability
Technology	Flexibility, future use
Supplier reliability and capability	Partnering costs, R&D access
Maintenance	Preventative maintenance
Inventory costs	Safety stock, storage costs
Transaction costs	Ease of transaction

Life cycle costs	Life of product
Opportunity costs	Cost of money
Asset utilization	Reduce procedure time
Revenue improvement	Reduce length of stay
Other	Training costs, ease of use

For both buyers of healthcare goods and services as well as med tech marketers, understanding economic value to customers (EV) or total cost of ownership (TCO) is becoming increasingly important.

In practical terms, estimating EV or TCO comes down to looking at both positive and negative differences that a product or solution provides compared with the next best alternative. For this simple example of a ventilator, let us assume that there are two suppliers' solutions to compare—Ventilator A and Ventilator B. Assume that both solutions perform roughly the same. Ventilator A has a purchase price of $29,000, and ventilator B has a price of $34,500, about 19 percent more. However, a closer look at cost of ownership reveals the real value. Ventilator A has filters that need to be changed four times a year. Each filter costs $100. Ventilator B has filters as well, but they only have to be changed once per year and cost about $100 each. Ventilator A has a flow sensor that needs to be changed at least once over its estimated seven-year life. Ventilator B uses a different technology and will not need to have a sensor changed. Due to the design, Ventilator A will require about $3,000 in annual maintenance costs. Ventilator B, on the other hand, will require about $2,500 in annual maintenance costs. With these data, the total cost of ownership over a seven-year life can be estimated.

Table 3.6: Example Total Cost of Ownership Summary

Cost	Ventilator A	Ventilator B
Acquisition price	$29,000	$34,500
Maintenance (7 years)	$21,000	$17,500

Filters (7 years total)	$2,800	$700
Flow sensor	$900	$0
Total cost of ownership	$53,700	$52,700

Table 3.6 shows a summary of the total cost of ownership of the two solutions (28). While Ventilator A has a much lower purchase price, the higher costs to maintain and operate the equipment causes it to have a higher cost of ownership compared with Ventilator B.

Table 3.7: Ventilator Company B Analysis Compared to Company A

Feature (Facts/ data about product)	Benefit (What does it do for customer?)	Value formula (What is the word formula to calculate value?)	Quantified value (What is the quantified value?)	Source/ Data
Filter lasts longer	Requires fewer filters and changes	(Company A filter costs/yr) – (Company B filter costs/ yr) * 7 yrs	$2,800 - $700 = $2,100	Workflow study
Lower maintenance requirements	Lower costs and down time	(Company A maintenance costs/ yr) – (Company B maintenance costs/ yr) * 7 yrs	$21,000 - $17,500 = $3,500	Estimated
New flow sensor technology	No need to replace sensor	# of Company A sensor changes over equipment life * cost/sensor	1* $900 = $900	Estimated
Total economic value to customer $6,500				

Calculating potential value in a structured way is critical. The table above shows a simple framework for translating features and benefits into quantifiable value. The table is completed from the perspective of Ventilator B's company.

In this example, each of the features is translated into one or more benefits. Here, for example, the feature of filters lasting longer translates into significant value for Ventilator B's company. In summary, there appears to be $6,500 in total value created, compared with Ventilator A. So, in theory, a price difference lower than $6,500 would mean Company B would provide more value or a lower total cost of ownership.

This is a simplistic example. In practice, the medical technology company would need to consider whether to discount economic benefits that occur over time into present value terms. This would allow for an apples-to-apples comparison with the acquisition costs. Another consideration would be to review the variables and assumptions around value. It probably would be the case that certain segments of hospitals get a much bigger benefit than other segments. Finally, the medical technology company would need to consider how much of the value to share with the customer to induce purchase.

Step 5: Confirm and validate.

Depending on what value is created and who value is created for, the confirmation or validation of value could take on different forms. Take the case of GHDX. One of the challenges diagnostic companies face is to not only prove that the diagnostic is accurate and provides meaningful insights, but also that it will influence some change in clinical practice. Payers would view an expensive new test as just adding costs if there is no resultant change in clinical practice. From a payer perspective, the payer is worse off if it pays for an expensive diagnostic test and doctors do not follow the test results (29).

So GHDX went a step further. They entered into risk-sharing arrangements where they tracked, along with a payer, whether the test was having the intended impact on clinical practice. If the number of patients receiving chemotherapy exceeded an agreed-upon threshold, even if the test suggested that the patients would not benefit, the insurer received a pre-negotiated lower price.

The case of GHDX is an example in the medical technology field of companies validating or confirming value through guarantees of some form. What are other forms of validating the value provided? Clinical and economic studies also provide a means of proving value. Real-world registries also provide a potential mechanism to prove clinical value.

Value and Segmentation

The previous section dealt with calculating value. One of the challenges in most business-to-business markets is often thinking through how value differs by segment. This challenge is even greater in the medical technology industry because of the complexities related to reimbursement systems. There are many different ways to segment markets in order to think about value. For simplicity, in the context of value, there are the following ways to think about segmentation:

- *Patient subgroups:* Medical devices and diagnostics have different effects on various patient subpopulations. This could be due to patient characteristics like existing co-morbidities, the type of surgical technique being used, or other factors. This often means the clinical and economic value will be different across patient subpopulations. Drug-eluting stents provide an example. While drug-eluting stents show an improvement in outcomes versus bare metal stents in all patient subgroups, the value of the technology is greater for certain patient subpopulations. These include diabetic patients, patients with small coronary vessels, and patients with long coronary lesions (30).

- *Provider segments:* Often, providers will value technologies differently depending on the type of institution. For example, a large teaching hospital may value a new technology differently than a small rural community hospital. This could be due to the mix of patients, the type of services offered, the operating characteristics, and the capabilities of the institution. Whether a provider is government owned, not-for-profit, or for-profit also influences behavior. Studies show that for-profit providers are more responsive to service line profitability changes than not-for-profit or government-owned providers (31).

- *Physician/user segments:* Even within a given physician specialty, different segments of users may have differing needs and value medical technologies differently. For example, a new surgical device that makes a certain type of surgery easier may be valued differently based on the physicians' skill level, specialized training, and years of experience.

Conclusion

Understanding value is the foundation of pricing for medical technologies. Value has three dimensions—clinical, economic, and psychological. While psychological value is certainly real and should be considered in pricing, the reality is that economic and clinical value is the foundation of the value equation for medical technologies. Increasingly, stakeholders are using economic and clinical value to assess medical technologies. So, it is important that medical technology companies themselves understand the value that their solutions bring.

NOTES

1. Anderson, J., Jain, D., and Chintagunta, P. (1993) Customer Value Assessment in Business Markets: A State-of-Practices Study. Journal of Business-to-Business Marketing 1:3-29

2. Cutler, D., and McClellan, M. (2001) Is Technological Change In Medicine Worth It? Health Affairs 20 (5): 11

3. Drummond, M., O'Brien, B., Stoddart, G., and Torrance, G. (1997) Methods for the Economic Evaluation of Health Care Programmes New York and Toronto: Oxford Medical Publications.

4. Christensen, C., Grossman, J., and Hwang, J. (2009) The Innovators Prescription. New York, NY: McGraw Hill.

5. Nagle, T. T., and Hogan, J. E. (2006). The strategy and tactics of pricing: A guide to growing profitably (4th ed.): Prentice Hall Upper Saddle River, NJ.

6. Hodgson, J. et al (2004) Drug-Eluting Stent Task Force: Final Report and Recommendations of the Working Committees on Cost-Economics, Access to Care, and Medicolegal Issues. Catheterization and Cardiovascular Interventions 62:1–17

7. Black, WC., (1990) The CE Plane: a Graphic Representation of Cost-Effectiveness. Med Decis. Mak. 10:212-14

8. Wikipedia.com, accessed June 28, 2012

9. Drummond, M., O'Brien, B., Stoddart, G., and Torrance, G. (1997) Methods for the Economic Evaluation of Health Care Programmes New York and Toronto: Oxford Medical Publications.

10. IBID

11. IBID

12. IBID

13. Hlatky, M., Sanders, G., and Owens, D. (2005) Evidence-Based Medicine And Policy: The Case Of The Implantable Cardioverter Defibrillator. Health Aff January 2005 vol. 24 no. 1 42-51

14. Briggs, A., O'Brien, B., and Blackhouse, G., Thinking Outside the Box: Recent Advances in the Analysis and Presentation of Uncertainty in Cost-Effectiveness Studies. Annu. Rev. Public Health 2002. 23:377-401

15. IBID

16. IBID

17. Shiroiwa, T., et. al. (2010) International survey on willingness-to-pay (WTP) for one additional QALY gained: what is the threshold of cost effectiveness? Health Econ. Apr; 19 (4) 422-37

18. Decision Memo for Screening Computed Tomography Colonography (CTC) for Colorectal Cancer. www.cms.gov. accessed June 28, 2012

19. Drummond, M., O'Brien, B., Stoddart, G., and Torrance, G. (1997) Methods for the Economic Evaluation of Health Care Programmes New York and Toronto: Oxford Medical Publications.

20. The idea for this chart was partially derived from: Briggs, A., O'Brien, B., and Blackhouse, G., Thinking Outside the Box: Recent Advances in the Analysis and Presentation of Uncertainty in Cost-Effectiveness Studies. Annu. Rev. Public Health 2002. 23:377-401, and Christensen, C., Grossman, J., and Hwang, J. (2009) The Innovators Prescription. New York, NY: McGraw Hill.

21. Hatcher, I., (2004) "Reducing Sharps Injuries Among Health Care Workers: A Sharps Container Quality Improvement Project," The Joint Commission Journal on Quality Improvement, July 2004 (vol. 28, no. 9)

22. See vanishpoint.com, accessed June 28, 2012

23. Details can be found in : www.mayoclinic.com/health/stroke/ds00150/dsection=causes

24. Whiteley, W., Tseng, M., and Sandercock, P. (2008) Blood Biomarkers in the Diagnosis of Ischemic Stroke - A Systematic Review. Stroke. 2008;39:2902-2909.

25. Cohen DJ, Bakhai A, Shi C, Githiora L, Lavelle T, Berezin RH, Leon MB, Moses JW, Carrozza JP, Zidar JP, Kuntz RE. (2004) Cost-effectiveness of sirolimus-eluting stents for treatment of complex coronary stenoses: Results from the SIRIUS trial. Circulation 2004;110:508-514.

26. Hornberger J, Cosler LE, Lyman GH. (2005) Economic analysis of targeting chemotherapy using a 21-gene RT-PCR assay in lymph-node-negative, estrogen-receptor-positive, early-stage breast cancer. m J Manag Care. 2005 Aug;11(8):476.

27. Ferrin, B., Plank, R. (2002) Total cost of ownership models: an exploratory study. Journal of Supply Chain Management. June, 2002.

28. Herbert, J. (2003) Total Cost of Ownership on Hospital Equipment. South African Federation of Hospital Engineering. March 2003. Accessed January 17, 2011.

29. Carlson, J., Garrison, L., and Sullivan, S. (2009) Paying for Outcomes: Innovative Coverage and Reimbursement Schemes for Pharmaceuticals. Journal of Managed Care Pharmacy. October, 2009

30. Firth, B., Cooper, L., and Fearn, S., (2008) The Appropriate Role Of Cost-Effectiveness In Determining Device Coverage: A Case Health Affairs, 27, no.6 (2008):1577-1586

31. Horwitz, J., (2005) Making Profits And Providing Care: Comparing Nonprofit, For-Profit, And Government Health Affairs, 24, no.3 (2005):790-801

CHAPTER 4

DEFINING A PRICING STRATEGY

Strategy is about choice. It is about deciding where to play and how to win. Pricing strategy is a critical element of the strategic choices a company needs to make. In order to be right, pricing strategy needs to be aligned with and support the overall marketing and business strategy. Unfortunately, the pricing strategy is often not explicitly chosen or is a last-minute decision. This often leads to missed growth opportunities, lost profits, upset customers, or other issues.

The previous chapter dealt with understanding value. For pricing strategy to be effective, it starts with a basic understanding of value. With this in hand, a firm can then begin to think about the right pricing strategy. Value is a necessary input into the strategy process but alone is not sufficient. There are a number of other critical inputs to making the right strategy choices.

Overview of Medical Technology Pricing Strategy

Key Inputs
Let us start with the basics inputs to a pricing strategy. In a typical business-to-business setting, there would be a number of inputs to consider

as part of setting a pricing strategy. These would include costs, competition, channel dynamics, firm and industry capacity, product life cycle, and customer value. However, for medical technology companies, this is just a starting point.

Because of the way technologies are paid for through reimbursement systems and due to other unique aspects of the industry, there are other inputs to consider as well. These include reimbursement, impact to stakeholders, ethical issues, and company image. For example, medical technology companies need to consider both how reimbursement will impact pricing strategy as well as consider how a pricing choice will impact reimbursement. Sometimes, particularly for new technologies, the choice of price level will impact a company's ability to gain reimbursement. In some markets, a high price will mean no reimbursement. In other markets, a high price will mean the chance for incremental reimbursement. Figure 4.1 provides an overview of the critical inputs to pricing strategy.

Figure 4.1 – Inputs to Pricing Strategy

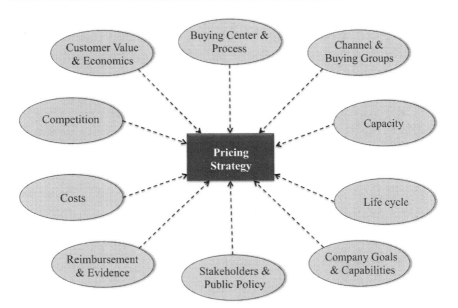

Smart pricing strategy starts with asking the right que:
each of the key inputs. Here are some generic questions to st

1. Costs:
   - What is the cost to manufacture product and serve customers?
   - Which costs are fixed and which are variable?
   - Do costs vary widely across segments?
   - How will costs change over time?
   - How do our costs compare with competition?

2. Channel/buying groups:
   - Who are key channel partners, and how will pricing affect their economics?
   - Who are key intermediaries or buying groups, and how does pricing strategy impact them?
   - How should buying groups be considered in the pricing strategy?

3. Capacity:
   - What is our capacity to manufacture product, and how does it compare with potential demand at different price points?
   - What is industry capacity? Is it increasing or decreasing?
   - Are there other capacity constraints to consider such as physician or customer training?

4. Competition:
   - Who are the competitors?
   - How might competitors respond to your pricing choice?
   - What are the competitor strengths and weaknesses?

5. Customer value and economics:
   - How will customers assess value?
   - What is economic value relative to next best alternative?

- How does value vary across segments, markets, and countries?
- What level of unmet need exists?
- What evidence is needed to substantiate customer value?
- What are the implications for provider and physician economics?

6. Reimbursement and evidence:
    - Will price level impact ability to gain new reimbursement?
    - Will price level impact ability to gain market access?
    - What level of evidence is needed to support reimbursement?
    - Will investments in evidence allow for higher reimbursement? If so, what is return on investment?
    - How will better evidence impact price of the technology?

7. Company capabilities and goals:
    - What kind of investment will the company make in generating clinical and economic evidence?
    - What level of marketing investment is being considered?
    - How does the company compare to competition in other non-product areas?
    - What are the business and marketing goals?

8. Stakeholders and public policy:
    - How will pricing strategy be viewed by the public?
    - How will pricing be viewed by policymakers?
    - Are there ethical issues to consider?
    - How will the technology impact government budgets?

9. Product life cycle:
   - Where is the product in the technology life cycle?
   - What is the nature of buyer demand and price sensitivity in the phase of the life cycle?

10. Buying center and process:
    - Who is in the buying center for this product or service?
    - What is the relative influence of each member of the buying center?
    - What will drive price sensitivity?
    - How does the buying center make decisions?

There are ten broad categories of inputs. Not all inputs will apply in every situation. However, failure to consider a critical input for the specific strategy under consideration could create a significant problem. The questions above are meant as thought starters and are by no means exhaustive.

Basic Strategic Pricing Process

It is helpful to provide an overview of the process of building a pricing strategy in order to better understand the inputs, process, and outputs. At a high level, the company should go through and analyze the relevant inputs as described in the previous section. In not all cases will it be required to gather all of the inputs listed. However, the company should make an assessment of the relevant inputs and then gather and analyze those inputs.

Once the company has gathered the relevant inputs, then it will need to develop, test, and refine the pricing strategy. This is where managerial judgment, the right analytics, and asking the right questions come into play. The output of the strategy process should be a number of deliverables. These include the choice of the pricing strategy as well as other key elements of pricing strategy. The outputs of the strategy process should include:

- *Pricing strategy*: There should be a conscious choice of whether the pricing strategy is skim, penetration, or neutral.

- *Target markets and segments*: The company should make choices about which markets and segments to serve and the pricing strategy for each.
- *Basic pricing structure*: Elements of the basic price structure should include the list price, target price, and floor price.
- *Price fences and metrics*: Thought should be given to the way to fence off markets and the metrics used to meter value to the customer.

It is not unusual for med tech companies to be organized in a way that the strategic price-setting process is managed separately from the price discounting or controlling process. If the deliverables above are developed by a group that has a global view in the company, this can help to avoid potential pricing issues across markets and ensure a thoughtful global approach. This does not mean that there needs to be a consistent global strategy. It only means that there is a thoughtful approach about setting global strategy and that trade-offs across markets can be made. The remainder of the chapter will focus on each of the strategic pricing deliverables outlined above.

Basic Pricing Strategies

There are three generic pricing strategies. These are skim pricing, penetration pricing, and neutral pricing. Choosing the right strategy requires careful analysis of the key inputs. The choice of a pricing strategy for a medical technology does not have to be uniform across countries. The same product can have different strategies in different counties. However, it is often wise to coordinate strategies across markets so as to not create price referencing, gray trade, or other issues.

Skim Pricing

Skim pricing is a strategy of setting prices relatively high compared to other alternatives, adjusting for value (1). The goal is to target the segment of customers who highly value your offering and have a high willingness to pay. In the medical technology industry, a skim strategy could also be a choice to target a specific indication or use of the technology that has much greater value than the average of all the indications. In skim pricing, often there is a conscious choice to forgo a chance at higher volume and limit focus on only certain buyers and segments.

There could be a number of reasons for choosing a skim strategy. A company may have a manufacturing capacity constraint and intentionally set the price high to limit demand. Alternatively, it could be a technology that is early in the life cycle and the company believes that demand will be price inelastic. In other words, the company believes that lowering the price will not increase market demand.

Reimbursement could be a reason for choosing a skim strategy. In some markets, reimbursement is cost based and the system has special reimbursement mechanisms for high-priced technologies. Usually, the hurdle for qualifying for this "add-on" payment is very high in terms of clinical evidence required as well as the cost of the technology. In this case, the wrong pricing strategy could lead to not being qualified for special reimbursement.

Fear of potential reaction of competitors could also be a reason to choose a skim strategy. It could be that the company is entering a market with a competitor who has a history of competing on price. The company may be fearful that a different pricing strategy would lead to competitive reaction and a price war. There are a number of potential reasons for choosing a skim strategy. It is often a safe place to start. While there is a chance that you will forgo volume, as we will discuss in the next section, it is often one of the right choices in many phases of the technology life cycle.

Penetration Pricing

Penetration pricing is setting the price of the offering at a relatively low price in order to rapidly grow volume and share (2). In this strategy, pricing is used as an area of focus in the marketing mix. Typically, this strategy is used when a company believes that demand will be price elastic and that lower prices will result in an increase in demand.

This is also a strategy that is used by price-based competitors to try to capture market share. The goal in this case is to use price to steal customers from competitors. It is a risky strategy since it assumes that competitors will not react or that if they do react, the company with the penetration pricing strategy will have a long-term cost advantage to survive a prolonged price war.

In many healthcare markets, demand is derived or is constrained by the reimbursement system. Derived demand simply means that the demand for the good or service is derived from some upstream activity. Likewise, many reimbursement systems artificially constrain demand through coding, coverage, and payment. This will be discussed in greater detail in chapter eight. Given the nature of demand and the payment system, using a penetration pricing strategy often results in stealing share from competitors and not growing overall demand.

Neutral Pricing

Finally, neutral pricing is setting the price so that it is somewhere close to competition or alternatives, adjusting for value differences. Usually, this strategy is chosen to deemphasize price in the purchase decision and to emphasize other buying factors. The basis of competition becomes something other than price. The competitive environment, product life cycle, cost position, and level of differentiation often lead companies to choose this strategy.

Understanding the Nature of Demand

While the concepts of skim, penetration, and neutral pricing strategies are relatively simple, experience suggests that many in the medical technology industry fail to explicitly choose a pricing strategy or pick the wrong strategy for their circumstances. This is often due to not considering the right inputs, misreading competition, or because they misunderstand the nature of demand.

In much of healthcare, in many markets, demand is derived. This means that demand is created by upstream activities like surgery schedules and emergency room visits. If a company lowers the price of sutures or surgical gowns, this will not induce an increase in overall market demand for sutures or surgical gowns. The company that lowers the price may be able to steal market share from competitors in the short term, but the overall market demand will not increase.

In some markets and circumstances, demand for a particular technology or service is constrained by reimbursement funding and coverage decisions. If a payer decides there is not enough evidence to cover and pay for a given technology, the price often has little impact on the decision to use the technology. The constraining factor is the coverage decision and not the price.

In other situations, companies have to negotiate price-volume arrangements with countries directly. These arrangements specify a sales volume threshold and a corresponding price. Any sales above the threshold are reimbursed at a reduced price. In this case, there is a pre-negotiated price-volume arrangement that impacts the relationship between price and demand. This usually only applies to expensive, new technologies that may have a significant budget impact to the payer. Understanding the nature of demand is a key part of making the right pricing strategy choices.

Price Strategy Case Study: Drug-Eluting Coronary Stents

In order to help illustrate the concepts of these basic pricing strategies, we will use the example of drug-eluting stents (DES). For simplicity, this example takes the perspective of the payer, and assumes that payment rates can be altered quickly. In reality, it usually takes time for the payer to adjust payment rates. In addition, a medical technology company will need to consider pricing from multiple perspectives—payer, provider, and user.

The first drug-eluting stent that was launched in the US was from Cordis Corporation. At the time of the launch, there was an existing market in place for bare metal stents. As was discussed in chapter three, DES represented a significant improvement in patient care and costs. At the time of launch of DES, bare metal stents, the next best alternative, sold for roughly $1,000 per stent. The other non-product costs for the two stenting procedures is roughly equivalent.

As was discussed in chapter three, the value of the new drug-eluting stent was relatively clear. For every one hundred patients treated with a DES, the payers would save roughly $2,475 per patient, excluding the incremental cost of the DES. Since cardiac stenting procedures averaged 1.4 stents per patient, the value created per stent for DES would be approximately $1,800 (3).

Figure 4.2 below shows a simple value map. This is a visual representation of price and value positioning. For the DES example, a price of approximately $2,800 would be a "neutral" price compared with bare metal stents. This is from a payer's perspective. This is because the price of the DES would be the cost of the bare metal stent plus the per-stent value created by the DES—approximately $1,800 per stent. A much higher price, let us say $3,600, would represent a skim pricing strategy since it is well above the value provided. Likewise, a much lower price, such as $2,000, would represent penetration pricing strategy.

Figure 4.2 – Drug-Eluting Stents (DES) Economic Value Map

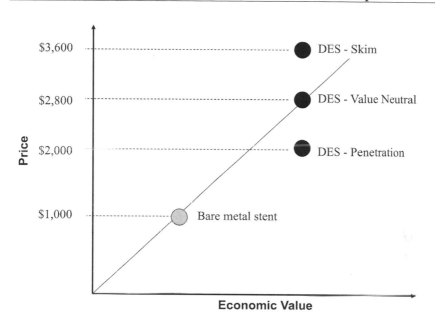

In the case of the stent pricing, Cordis chose a neutral pricing strategy since the company launched DES at a list price of $3,200 and average selling price of roughly $2,800 per stent (4). Beyond economic benefits, the technology had other clinical and psychological benefits. One of the psychological benefits was the reduction in the need of repeat procedures. This meant that patients and their families had a lower chance of having to go through the ordeal of a major medical procedure in the future.

What would make a company choose a skim pricing strategy? Going back to the decision inputs, there could be a variety of reasons a med tech company might choose a skim pricing strategy. Using the DES example above, let's assume that the company had a limited manufacturing capacity and could only supply a small segment of the available market. In this case, the company might want to "limit" demand by purposefully choosing a skim pricing strategy.

Alternatively, the initial variable costs to manufacture the technology may be extremely high, and the company will be in a position of losing money on each unit sold below a certain price. This may cause the company to choose a skim strategy. Another reason to chose a skim strategy could be related to reimbursement. The company may believe that a skim strategy will help support establishment of the right reimbursement levels in some markets.

Why might a company choose a penetration strategy? In this case, the company would be trying to make pricing a key decision criteria for purchases. It could be that the company believes it has a sustainable long-term cost advantage. Alternatively, perhaps the company is first to market with a new technology and believes that it will have a short window to penetrate the market before competition arrives. In general, a penetration pricing strategy is one to be careful with. Competition can respond quickly, and price wars often can result with an adverse impact on industry economics.

Why might a company choose a value-neutral pricing strategy? It could be that the company is concerned about how competition might respond. Take the example of the Cordis DES launch. What if the company chose a penetration pricing strategy? There was a large and established bare metal stenting market already in place. For certain patient subgroups, the existing technology was a viable alternative. A penetration pricing strategy for DES, such as a price of $2,000, might have caused bare metal stent manufacturers to react by lowering their prices.

In this case, as shown in figure 4.3, a penetration pricing strategy could have caused a shift in the economic value equivalency line down. In other words, a lower DES price may have caused bare metal stent prices to be lowered. This could have resulted in the penetration pricing strategy being neutralized by the bare metal stent price reaction. While DES was a technological improvement and a new class of products, bare metal stents were a clear alternative and a comparator. Thus, in this example, DES prices would have to be lowered again to gain the position of penetration pricing.

Figure 4.3 – Shift in Economic Value Equivalency

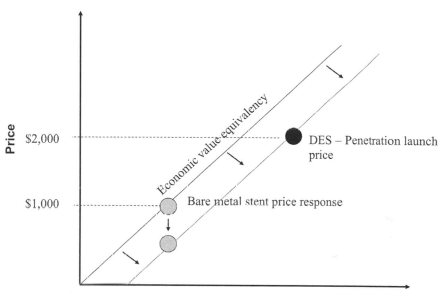

This is a simplistic example to illustrate the concept. The reality is that the strategy choice becomes more complex due to the various stakeholders involved, the payment system, and the value differences across segments. Now that you have a understanding of the three basic pricing strategies, let us move on to how product life cycle impacts pricing strategy. Picking the right general strategy for a medical technology requires an understanding of the product life cycle concept.

Pricing Over Technology Life Cycle

Classically, any product or technology goes through a life cycle with four phases. These stages can be visualized in the example s-curve in Figure 4.4. Technologies passes through stages of introduction, growth, maturity, and decline. Understanding buyer behavior and industry dynamics throughout the life cycle is critical for selecting the right pricing strategy and adapting the strategy over time.

Figure 4.4 – Typical S-Curve Product Life cycle

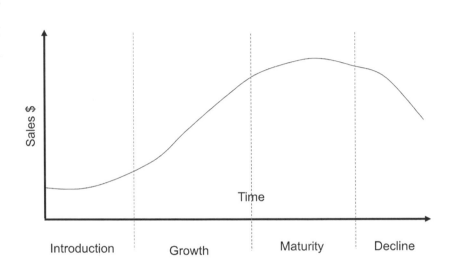

Introductory Phase

The introductory phase is usually a phase where there is relatively little direct competition. It also tends to be a phase where the primary customers are the innovators and early adopters. These customer segments tend to be technically savvy and are often considered thought leaders. They are willing to takes risks (5). From a pricing standpoint, these customers are less price sensitive since they are interested more in breaking new ground and being out in front of the pack. In the medical technology market, key opinion leaders are often the early adopters and advocates of the technology.

For medical technology companies, the introductory phase also presents some unique challenges. The introductory phase is one in which the innovative company is usually still building the full picture of the value of a new technology. This is because once a product is approved and launched, the companies are often still conducting clinical trials to fully understand the value of the new technology or are exploring its use in other indications. So the full value of the technology may not be fully understood at launch.

In addition, the other key consideration at this stage is reimbursement. The reimbursement systems vary around the world. In some countries, the reimbursement system is largely a cost-based system. This means that new innovations need to cost a significant amount in order to potentially qualify for additional reimbursement. In other markets, payers will look at the budget impact of a technology and its value across patient segments. Payers in these markets may seek to limit use of a new technology to specific patient groups or indications.

Lastly, a key consideration in this stage is establishing a new market. New technologies such as drug-eluting stents and molecular diagnostics create new markets. In doing so, they also establish the value reference for future innovations. This means that choosing the wrong pricing strategy and price level could not only impact the current innovation, but also all innovations that follow. Future innovations will use the initial innovation as the comparator.

Take the cardiac reperfusion marketplace and how it developed over time. First, balloon angioplasty was developed as a solution to treat clogged arteries. In this procedure, a balloon mounted on a catheter is inserted in a patient's femoral artery. The balloon travels over the catheter to the site of the blockage in one of the patient's cardiac arteries. Once at the site of the blockage, the balloon is inflated and the plaque is pressed against the artery walls, thus opening the vessel.

A certain number of patients had the artery immediately close after the balloon was removed. This created a serious patient safety issue. Likewise, a certain percentage of patients' arteries reclogged over time. In order to solve these two issues, bare metal stents were invented. These stents were usually mounted on the balloon, and the procedure was essentially the same. In the stenting procedure, the stents were expanded when the balloon opened and stayed in place in the artery.

Like with the balloon angioplasty procedures, a certain percentage of the stent patients had their arteries reclogged. In order to combat the reclogging, drug-eluting stents were developed. These were stents that were coated with a drug to help prevent the process of reclogging. These new

DES represented a significant advancement over stenting. Likewise, stenting represented a significant advancement over balloon angioplasty.

So, in each case, from balloon angioplasty to stents and from stents to drug-eluting stents, the comparator or value reference became the technology that came before it, along with the procedure and follow-up costs. Therefore, when prices were set for the balloon angioplasty technology, they also helped establish the comparator or value reference for each successive generation of technology advancement that came along.

What does all this mean for pricing during the introductory phase? A review of the key decision inputs gives some insights. Table 4.1 provides a summary of the key decision inputs and the implications for the pricing strategy. In reviewing these inputs, it is clear that most of the inputs would suggest the company follow a skim or neutral pricing strategy during the introductory phase. Common sense also helps support this position. It is relatively easy to lower the price of a medical technology as opposed to increase the price after launch. Common sense would dictate that, when in doubt, it is best to choose a skim strategy at this phase.

Table 4.1: Example Introductory Phase Inputs

Key Input	Implications for Pricing Strategy	Best Strategy
Value	• Value is usually not fully understood across all indications at launch • May be creating reference value for future technologies	Skim/neutral
Costs	• Typically manufacturing costs are higher at launch of a new technology and decline over the technology life cycle. This is called the experience curve effect. • Costs to serve may be high during introduction phase	Skim
Capacity	• New technologies sometimes have manufacturing capacity constraints • Physician training could be a constraint as well	Skim/neutral

Reimbursement	• Lower costs may dissuade the creation of special reimbursement payments	Skim
Competition	• Might want to set umbrella for competition to come under	Skim/neutral
Buyer behavior/price sensitivity	• Usually targeting innovators and early adopters with low price sensitivity	Skim

Growth Phase

During the growth phase, more customers become adopters of the technology. At this stage, the early-majority and late-majority categories of adopters enter. These segments tend to be more cautious than early adopters. They are also looking for proof and may be pressured into adoption for economic reasons or peer pressure (6). In the medical technology world, these categories of adopters may be seeking more evidence of the effectiveness and safety of a given innovation. They may also be getting pressure to adopt the technology to remain current with leading treatments. These groups tend to be more price sensitive than the early adopters.

Since the early majority and late majority account for a large percentage of the population, this period is characterized by rapid growth. Also, during this stage, a company's average costs are probably declining as it becomes more experienced at manufacturing the technology. It may also see a decline in cost to serve as it gains experience and scale in serving customers. From an industry perspective, new competitors may be entering the market, and overall demand is growing. At this point in the life cycle, companies usually adopt a neutral or penetration strategy. As was discussed previously, it is important to consider the nature of demand when considering the pricing strategy.

Maturity Phase

This phase is characterized by slowing demand. The only adopter category left is the laggards. These users are very skeptical of innovation and show no thought leadership (7). The markets are usually crowded with many competitors at this point. While there may be innovation, it usually is minor incremental improvements. Most customers at this point tend to be familiar with the technology and are able to begin to push on suppliers for price concessions since they do not need to rely as much on suppliers for training and expertise.

It is at this point in the life cycle that there is a danger of price wars breaking out. Since the only way for companies to grow is to take share from someone else, the temptation to use price as a lever grows. Companies at this point should adopt a neutral or skim pricing strategy. Without a sustainable long-term cost advantage, penetration strategy means the company may find itself in a price war that shrinks the overall market.

Decline Phase

At this point in the product life cycle, the market has peaked and is declining. It could also be a period where the number of competitors shrinks. This could be due to industry consolidation as well as companies leaving the marketplace. Since there is no growth, pursuing a penetration or low-price strategy at this point will only result in stealing share from competition. Alternatively, if competitors decides to defend their share position, they will lower prices, and the result will be a price war. So at this point in the product life cycle, it is best to pursue a neutral or skim strategy.

Price Range and Levels

In practical terms, when a med tech company goes through a process of developing a pricing strategy and setting prices, it usually is an iterative process. Once relative value is understood and the key inputs are gathered, the company can then make an informed decision. Usually this involves some sensitivity analysis and financial modeling around a potential range of prices.

Broadly speaking, the possible price levels could fall within the range, as shown in Figure 4.5. The top of the range is the total value. This represents the economic, clinical, and psychological value. The bottom of the range is some price that reflects the minimum acceptable margin the company would like to earn.

Figure 4.5 – Possible Price Range

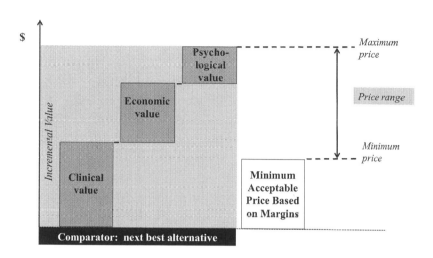

Value sets the top of the range, and costs set the bottom of the range. Often the range is fairly wide. This is where the company has to make a pricing strategy choice based on an assessment of all of the available inputs. At this stage of the pricing process, the goal is not to be too precise, but rather to settle on a price level range that is about right. The company can refine the price level and optimize the strategy through an iterative process.

Evaluating the other inputs should help provide some direction. For example, there may be a wide range between the price at an acceptable margin and the total value of a given medical technology. However, if the company determines that there will be a manufacturing capacity issue for a couple of years, it will need to factor capacity into the pricing decision. An excess of demand over supply may mean that the company should choose a skim strategy and set the price higher within the range to intentionally limit demand.

The output of the pricing process at this stage is a general pricing strategy and a preliminary pricing level to further refine. In addition, the outputs should include decisions such as:

- The countries and segments to target
- The offering strategy for each target country and segment
- The pricing strategy for each target country and segment
- The target price level for each country and segment

At this point, the company will need to make some tough decisions. For example, there may be some countries where it does not make sense to launch the product. This could be due to the healthcare system, market dynamics, or the investment required to bring the product to market. There may be some countries where the product has to be niched because the price needs to be set at a high level for that market to avoid price referencing to other markets.

The company will also need to sometimes make difficult choices on target patient populations for the technology. This often occurs when the value of the technology varies widely across patient populations. It may be the case that health technology assessments or buyer behavior causes the technology to be targeted to specific patient populations. The company needs to evaluate the desire for broad patient access and the long-term financial consequences of pricing decisions.

It is also at this point that some simple scenario modeling would be helpful. Scenario modeling is a management tool that allows for greater insights into the risks and potential implications of strategy decisions. It allows for modeling strategic choices against alternative views of the future to understand the potential implications. In a scenario model for pricing, the team would develop three or four alternative views of the future. It could be a very easy future where there is robust reimbursement. Alternatively, it could be a very difficult future where customers are under extreme cost pressure. With these scenarios defined, buyer behavior and competitive reaction can be modeled. This is often a helpful tool when there is a high degree of uncertainty about the future market environment.

The choice of the pricing strategy should lead to a general range of price levels. The question then becomes: Within the given range, what is the appropriate price level? This is sometimes a difficult question to answer. It requires understanding the price sensitivity drivers. Refining and optimizing the pricing strategy and price level requires answering some critical questions:

- Given the pricing strategy (skim, neutral, penetration), what is the range of price levels to consider?
- How are the various price levels within the range impacted by customer price sensitivity drivers?
- How do various price points within the desired range impact volume assumptions?
- How will profitability be impacted at various price levels?
- How can different prices across markets or segments be fenced off?
- Are there any price referencing issues to consider?
- Are there health policy and reimbursement issues to consider?
- How will competition respond?
- What are alternative future market scenarios, and what are the implications for the pricing strategy?

The output of refining and optimizing the price level should be greater precision on what the final price level should be. Additionally, a key output should be refined price levels by segment. Since the value and price sensitivity factors will often vary by segment, the company should perform the analysis by segment and use managerial judgment to refine the price levels. The final product should be a well-thought-out pricing strategy and price levels for each target segment.

Price Structure, Fences, and Metrics

Basic Price Structure

At this point, the company will also need to decide on a basic price structure. The basic structure is simply deciding on list price, the type and nature of discounts, target price, and a floor price (8). If you were building a house, the basic house structure would be the foundation and framing of the house. It is what ultimately helps shape the appearance of the house.

Likewise, the pricing structure is ultimately what helps shape the customer's perception of price.

The pricing structure could be very simple. For example, a company selling a new disposable medical device used in outpatient surgery may decide that it does not want to offer any discounts initially. In this case, the company would set a list price that is also its target price and offer no discounts. This a very simple form of a price structure.

In most circumstances, the company will choose to define some form of discounts to drive the right customer behavior and take advantage of varying willingness to pay. Since many purchases in healthcare are increasingly being influenced by professional buyers, customers have grown accustomed to negotiating quantity and other discounts. Without a basic price structure that includes some form of discounting, the company will be in a difficult position when negotiating at the provider level.

The company will want to think carefully about the basic price structure. Often, selling the same product to different countries and segments means there are varying needs, willingness to pay, costs to serve, reimbursement, and other factors that will cause wide differences in price structure. Without a thoughtful approach to establishing the basic price structure, the company can end up with conflicting structures and many pricing and customer issues. For example, a company that sells products in Europe many find that the optimal price structure in one European country is significantly different than in a neighboring country. Without a strategic approach to establishing a basic price structure, the company could find that the price structure in the lower priced market creates a price referencing problem for the other country.

The choice of the basic pricing structure will depend on a variety of factors. The factors influencing the structure design are many and could include technology life cycle, variation in cost to serve, value, willingness to pay, market structure, competitive environment, customer buying behavior, target segments and countries, and reimbursement. This is why designing the basic structure should be thought of as a strategic pricing exercise. It requires a strategic and proactive approach to avoid mistakes.

Fences

The previous sections dealt with choosing the pricing strategy, refining the price levels for each segment, and deciding on a basic price structure. If prices are to vary across segments or markets, the company will need to establish fences to prevent prices from one segment or market from spilling over into another segment or market. A fence is a mechanism to charge different prices to different segments based on differing needs, behaviors, and operating characteristics. The fencing mechanism should be based on objective criteria.

As consumers, we encounter price fences all the time. The simplest example is to consider how airlines charge different prices to different consumers on the same flight. There are a number of ways that airlines charge different prices and fence those prices. One example is time of ticket purchase. In general, a fourteen-day advance ticket purchase will cost less than a ticket purchased two days before the flight. Class of service is also another fence. First class is charged a different price than coach class. Also, ticket restrictions is another way to vary the price and fence off different travelers. A businessperson may purchase an unrestricted coach-class ticket that allows the traveler to change flights. This ticket usually costs much more than a restricted coach-class ticket. Thus, airlines have found many ways to charge different prices for the same flight by fencing off segments by needs and objective criteria.

In the medical technology industry, there are a number of means to fence buyers. The typical approaches to fencing include:

- *Quantity purchase*: The total quantity purchased by the customer in units (e.g., tests, kits) or monetary value (e.g., dollars, euros) within a defined period of time. A customer who purchases six hundred thousand dollars' worth of a given supply annually from a vendor may be charged a different price than another who only buys fifty thousand dollars' worth annually. The company should use care in segmenting only on this criteria since hospital buying groups who consolidate spending across many hospitals can use volume as a leverage against suppliers.

- *Share of wallet*: This is the supplier's share of the customer's total purchases or procedures within a given category (e.g., sutures, tests, implants). As an example, a orthopedic implant supplier may charge a different price to a customer who buys 90 percent of its hip implant needs from the supplier than a customer who purchases 20 percent of its hip implant needs from the supplier.

- *Bundles purchased*: This is segmentation based on varying the price by the number of product lines or categories purchased. A customer who purchases all of the supplier's product lines may be eligible for different pricing than a customer who purchases only one product line.

- *Location*: Customers in one country or region of a country are eligible for different pricing based on the local dynamics and cost to serve. For example, two customers in Canada may be charged a very different rate for a service visit based on the location. A customer in Toronto may have a very different cost to serve than a customer in the far reaches of the Yukon Territory.

- *Product quality/design*: Different customers have differing needs in terms of the quality level sought or the operating needs. The supplier can segment based on needs and charge different prices for a different product or quality level. Consider a manufacturer of CT scanners. The manufacturer can have differing prices based on the software configuration that is used in the analysis or storage of CT scan images.

- *Service needs*: Different customer segments often have varying needs for service, support, and education. For example, a hospital that operates its clinical laboratory for three shifts, six days a week, would have different service needs than a customer that runs one shift six days a week.

- *Combination*: Often, companies choose a combination of the above variables to segment and fence buyers. For example, companies often choose to combine purchase quantity and share of wallet into a single segmentation and price fence approach.

Metrics

Price metrics are the means to capture customer value and define the unit of exchange. For example, a surgical glove manufacturer may sell gloves based on a per-glove price. This defines the unit of exchange. Medical technology companies sell goods and services using a variety of price metrics. These metrics include:

- *Price per unit*: A price is established per unit such as per surgical glove, per diagnostic test, per box of sutures, etc. This is the simplest form of a price metric.

- *Price per procedure*: Here, the manufacturer sets the price on a procedure basis. This could occur when there is one core technology that is used along with many different combinations of enabling technologies. For example, a hip implant supplier may choose to price per procedure. The hospital is charged a per-procedure price that covers the cost of the hip implant and all the enabling technologies that are used to implant the artificial hip.

- *Price per outcome*: Here, the manufacturer prices the product on an outcome basis. The outcome is measured in the customer's terms. In-vitro diagnostics is an example. In the diagnostics business, suppliers sell capital equipment, service, reagents, and consumables. Many of the manufacturers in the in-vitro diagnostics market offer a pricing option on a cost-per-reportable-result basis. There are some variants, but the supplier charges the hospital every time the hospital "reports" a test result. This charge includes the price of the equipment, service, reagents, and consumables. In this example, the supplier ends up taking on some risk since products are shipped to the customer and the customer reports back the reportable results. The supplier then needs to reconcile actual product usage required to produce a result. It is a complicated pricing metric, but customers like it since it aligns with how they are reimbursed. Customers also like it since it can transfer operational risk from the customer to the supplier.

- *Price per time period*: This pricing metric is to charge the customer a fixed charge per time period. This is often used in service pricing where customers are charged a fixed amount per month or year for various service levels. It can also be used for product pricing. In this case, the customer and supplier agree on a fixed charge per month and the parameters under which adjustments will be made to the fixed charge. For example, a supplier of packs and gowns may believe that it can drive down customers' overall usage of packs and gowns through an efficiency program. In this case, the supplier could set a fixed monthly fee and then work with the customer to reduce waste. The supplier is taking on the risk and betting that it can help the customer reduce waste. The supplier would need to set some parameters around the pricing metric, like procedure volume, to protect it against changes in the customers' business.

- *Price per patient per period of time*: In the pharmaceutical world, it is not uncommon to look at pricing as the price per patient over some period of time. This could be cost of therapy per month, for example. This usually involves medicines that are used to treat chronic conditions over some period of time. The same can hold true for certain medical technologies. For example, the home INR case study mentioned in chapter one looked at patient costs to the payer over a month or year.

Ideally, price metrics should consider the value brought to the customer, the cost to serve, and any strategic advantages the supplier's products or services have relative to the competition. The supplier also has to be careful to consider the risk that it assumes in moving to different pricing metrics as well as the administrative burden of reporting and tracking the different type of price metric.

Businesses with Capital Equipment and Follow-on Revenue

A number of segments of the med tech industry have capital equipment and follow-on revenue business models. These include in-vitro diagnostics, in-vivo diagnostics, and other parts of the industry. This is where capital equipment is sold, leased, rented, or given to the customer. After placement of the capital equipment, there is a follow-on stream of revenue from consumables, service, or other recurring revenue. In this case, the company has to make a strategic choice about how to price the different components of the offering and how to capture value.

There is no simple formula for how to price the capital versus the follow-on consumables and service revenue stream. Customers have gotten smart about looking at the total acquisition cost of capital, consumables, and service over a fixed period of time. Therefore, playing games by capturing more or less value through the capital versus the follow-on revenue streams is not often an opportunity to trick the customer. The customer will calculate the total cost of the contract over a fixed period of time.

There may be cases where there is a difference in assumptions about the length of time a customer will retain the capital. For example, customers may issue five-year tenders on average and calculate the total acquisition costs over a five-year period, whereas a supplier bidding on the tenders may determine that the customers will hold the equipment longer than five years. In this case, it may make sense to capture more value through the follow-on revenue stream and less through the capital component.

The supplier may also have some strategic advantage over the competition that allows it to use this through the offering strategy. It could be a major advantage in serviceability of the equipment, manufacturing costs, or other areas. In general, the company should consider a number of factors when determining how to price the different elements of the offering. The factors to consider are:

- *Substitutes*: The availability of substitutes for the follow-on revenue stream item will matter. For example, in parts of the medical imaging business, service represents a follow-on revenue stream for capital equipment manufacturers. However, customers can often access service through third-party service entities and not be required to use the manufacturer. Alternatively, in the in-vitro diagnostics industry, it is often the case that the equipment manufacturer is the only source for the reagents that are used to perform testing. Whether or not there is a lock-in to follow-on revenue will make a difference in how value is captured through capital and follow-on revenue sources.

- *Switching costs*: The degree of switching costs should dictate the strategy choice for how to capture value between the capital good and the follow-on revenue. If switching costs are high, the supplier may want to capture more value through the follow-on revenue, all things being equal.

- *Contract length*: If the contract length is relatively short, then the supplier will want to capture more value through the capital portion of the offering.

- *Costs*: Understanding the relative cost of the capital, service, and other offering components should influence the strategy for how to capture value.

- *Sources of competitive advantage*: The supplier should look to any specific sources of competitive advantage and take these into consideration in pricing the different components of the offering strategy. This could be in costs, serviceability of the equipment, upselling opportunities, or other areas. The source of competitive advantage could be in the value created by the different components of the offering. A suppler with capital equipment that is significantly differentiated in value from competition will want to consider this in the strategy.

- *Ability to monitor customer performance*: The decision to capture a large portion of the value through the follow-on revenue streams should consider the ability of the company to track and monitor customer purchasing commitments. A company that provides capital at a very low price in the hopes of making it up in follow-on revenue needs to have good processes in place to ensure that the follow-on revenue occurs.

There is often a temptation for companies with this business model, who have lower cost capital, to "give away" the capital component and try to capture value through the follow-on revenue streams. There are a number of issues with this approach. First, it conditions customers to always assume capital will be free. It also devalues the capital technology, and potentially the value-creating elements of the capital. Finally, it creates the need for robust processes to manage and monitor compliance to purchase requirements for the follow-on revenue components.

Medical Technology Price Sensitivity Drivers

In defining a pricing strategy and refining the price level, it is often helpful to consider factors that drive customer price sensitivity. Nagle and Hogan define a number of price/value sensitivity factors that should be considered in setting price levels and the value capture rate. While many of these factors apply in medical technology, there are additional ones and some finer nuances to the ones described by Nagle and Hogan (9). For the medical technology market, eleven price/value sensitivity drivers have been defined here. Not all of the drivers will play a role in each pricing decision. However, it would be prudent to consider these drivers in optimizing the pricing strategy and price level. The medical technology price sensitivity drivers to consider:

- *Clinical outcomes*: What is the impact of your product or solution on patient outcomes? Does your product or solution lead to an improvement in patient outcomes? How important are these improvements? These are all important questions to answer since products or solutions that can clearly demonstrate an improvement in clinical outcomes will have a much lower price sensitivity, all things being equal. In particular, any meaningful, statistically significant improvements in hard clinical endpoints will have much greater value and much lower price sensitivity.

- *Unmet need*: How satisfied are clinicians and patients with the current diagnostics and treatment options available? If they are relatively satisfied, there will be much higher relative price sensitivity. The unmet need could be clinical improvements, ease of use, compliance with existing therapy or diagnostics, or efficiency of using one technique or solution compared to another. Consider colorectal cancer screening. Currently, there are three primary methods that include stool tests, colonoscopy, and virtual colonoscopy using CT scan technology (10). Each of these methods is not ideal and suffers from concerns about convenience, costs, or compliance. Therefore, a new diagnostic such as a simple and accurate blood-based test would be able to meet a big unmet need and would have a relatively low price sensitivity.

- *Perceived outcome risk*: Buyers are more price sensitive when they perceive there is significant risk in being able to achieve the outcomes that will lead to the value promise of a technology or solution. This could be due to a number of factors such as the quality of evidence, the believability of the benefit claims, and the history of the company. For example, a vendor selling a software solution to a physician-owned chain of surgical centers may promise significant productivity benefits and labor savings. However, if there is a lack of compelling evidence to support the vendor's claims of value, the customer will likely discount the value promised and be more price sensitive. Likewise, a payer may be unwilling to reimburse a significant amount for a new diagnostic test not because it believes the test is not accurate, but because it believes physicians will not change clinical practice with insights from the test.

- *Budget impact*: How does the technology or solution impact the overall budget of the payer or provider? Technologies or services that have a much higher overall budget impact will have greater price sensitivity. For example, while the cost of individual sutures may be low, the total spending by the hospital operating room on sutures is a meaningful portion of its budget. Therefore, the operating room would be sensitive to the overall price of sutures. Budget impact should take into account the impact to the budget from a total cost of ownership perspective.

- *Procedure or service profitability*: At the provider level, the profitable of the service or procedure can drive price sensitivity. A procedure that is seen as unprofitable will likely be under focus. Any supply items or services that are used in performing the service will be more sensitive to price than items used in other procedures that are not in focus. Reimbursement and funding play a role in procedure or service profitability. A new technology that has no or limited incremental reimbursement would cause much greater price sensitivity. Therefore, the level of profitability of the procedure or service can impact price sensitivity.

- *Perceived purchase risk*: Whether the buying decision is a made by a physician, a laboratory director, or a hospital value analysis committee, humans are making the buying decision. This is where ego, career risk, time involvement, and cost to make a buying decision play a part in the process. In general, buyers will be more price sensitive in situations where they perceive less purchase risk. For example, buying surgical gauze will be perceived as less risky than making a buying decision on a new piece of capital equipment for the cardiac catheterization lab. In the former case, the purchaser will be much more willing to take risks.

- *Patient advocacy*: Certain diseases and conditions have very strong patient advocacy groups. These advocacy groups are active in public policy debates, in raising general awareness, and in focusing on finding cures and treatments to the disease or condition. In general, a disease or condition that has a very strong advocacy presence will have lower price sensitivity relative to other diseases or conditions without a strong presence. This, of course, will vary by country and region.

- *Physician/user specialty*: Different users or specialties have differing influence within the provider organizations where they perform procedures. This influences how sensitive they are to price and the relative influence on purchasing decisions. Different physician specialties also have varying degrees of price sensitivity due to the type and cost of supplies that they typical use. For example, a cardiothoracic surgeon may have a differing pricing sensitivity and influence in a provider organization than an ear, nose, and throat (ENT) specialist.

- *Aligned incentives*: Situations where the key influencer of the purchase decision is aligned economically with the purchase decisions will lead to greater price sensitivity. This alignment could be due to employment. For example, physicians employed by a hospital. It could also be due to ownership such as physicians' owning a surgical center. Where specific ownership or employment does not exist, special programs—like bundled payments and gain-sharing programs where physicians receive incentives to reduce hospital costs—play a role. Studies of gain-sharing programs and bundled payments in the US coronary stent market and orthopedic implant market show that these programs reduce technology prices and utilization (11).

- *Switching costs*: The cost to switch from one vendor or solution to another certainly can have an impact on price sensitivity. These switching costs can be for things such as training, change management, and compliance with the new process or technology.

For example, a hospital evaluating a new scheduling system for the operating room needs to consider the significant effort involved in training, change management, and gaining compliance with a new system. This switching cost would certainly impact price sensitivity.

- *Reference and fairness:* At the end of the day, value and price are perceived. This means that buyers view the price and value through a human lens. The issues of fairness and reference come into play. Buyers will be more sensitive to prices that are perceived as unfair or outside of a reasonable range compared to a reference. The reference could be prices of potential alternatives, the price of the same product in a different country, or the price of an earlier generation of the same technology. For example, most people involved in healthcare understand that the health systems, policies, health economics, and cost to serve vary widely from country to country. Therefore, there is some tolerance for price differences for the same product across counties. However, when the price differences go beyond a certain point, the issue of fairness and reasonableness come into play.

Conclusion

Strategy is about choice. In determining the pricing strategy, the company has a number of choices to make. This includes the pricing strategy for each target segment and market. It also includes choices about the price level, how to fence different prices across segments, and pricing metrics to use to capture value. This is best done by taking a holistic approach that considers a range of possible decision inputs. Value should be the foundation of the pricing strategy. Failure to make a conscious choice about pricing strategy could ultimately impact potential growth, profits, and company image.

NOTES

1. Adapted from Monroe, K., (2003) Making Profitable Decisions. (3rd ed.) McGraw-Hill. New York, NY.
2. IBID
3. Cohen DJ, Bakhai A, Shi C, Githiora L, Lavelle T, Berezin RH, Leon MB, Moses JW, Carrozza JP, Zidar JP, Kuntz RE. (2004) Cost-effectiveness of sirolimus-eluting stents for treatment of complex coronary stenoses: Results from the SIRIUS trial. Circulation 2004;110:508-514.
4. Associated Press. (2003) J&J Drops Price of New Cypher Heart Stent. September 8, 2003
5. Rodgers, E., (1995) Diffusion of Innovation. (4th ed.): The Free Press New York, NY.
6. IBID
7. IBID
8. Monroe, K., (2003) Making Profitable Decisions. (3rd ed.) McGraw-Hill. New York, NY.
9. Nagle, T. T., and Hogan, J. E. (2006). The strategy and tactics of pricing: A guide to growing profitably (4th ed.): Prentice Hall Upper Saddle River, NJ.
10. See WebMD.com, accessed June 28, 2012
11. Ketcham, J. and Furukawa, M., (2008) An ACE in the deck? Bundled-payment demo shows returns for hospitals, physicians, patients. Health Aff. May 2008 vol. 27 no. 3 803-812

CHAPTER 5

DEVELOPING AN OFFERING STRATEGY

An offering strategy is about making a conscious choice about how to serve different segments of customers to earn a profit. The customer segments can vary widely because of needs, behaviors, willingness to pay, cost to serve, and other factors. However, without a way to vary the offering to address the differences across segments, companies can end up in a situation where they are serving customers who are marginally profitable or, worse yet, unprofitable. One solution is to rethink the offering strategy.

An offering, as it is used here, means the core good or service, plus the surrounding services and business terms. The company has three dimensions to think about in designing the offering. First, it is the core product or service. Second, it is the surrounding support services. Finally, it is the business terms that govern the transaction. Having a clear offering strategy provides enormous flexibility to address the needs of different customer segments, while still earning a profit.

The offering strategy has another key advantage. This is in customer negotiations. With a single offering and no way to vary the value that is provided to customers, the company will have little flexibility, other than price, to meet different customer needs. However, with a flexible offering, the sales team will have the ability to trade off value for price. This flexibility becomes even more important when the product enters the mature phase of the technology life cycle where buyers are more willing to take purchasing risks.

Designing an Offering Strategy

An offering in the medical technology field usually consists of a core product as well as services. The core product can be a good such as a suture, capital equipment, or a disposable item. Increasingly, a core product can also include a combination of capital equipment and software. In many parts of the industry, such as in in-vivo diagnostics, software is an important part of the offering and is something that can easily be varied.

The other component of the offering is the surrounding services that are provided by the supplier. In the medical technology industry, there are a number of services that can be offered. These include items such as:

- Customer training
- Break fix service (service hours, response time, etc.)
- Delivery time
- Shipment frequency
- Telephone support
- Spare parts
- Process improvement
- Special consulting
- Consigning inventory
- Inventory management
- Customer start-up
- Technical support
- Co-development
- Clinical support

Obviously, a number of these services are critical for the customer to appropriately use the product for clinical care. As an example, a company selling a new digital pathology solution to a hospital laboratory will need to train the staff on how to use the technology. The question is not whether the company offers training, but how much training and whether it is the same level of training for a very large customer who purchases one million dollars' worth of equipment as opposed to a customer who purchases one hundred thousand dollars' worth of equipment.

It is also important to link the offering strategy to pricing. In the previous example of a large and small customer buying different digital pathology systems, it could be the case where the smaller customer actually has a higher absolute cost to serve because the customer is less sophisticated and needs to access customer support and training services more frequently. In this case, it is important to think through the offering strategy and how it is connected to the pricing strategy.

There are three broad combinations to think about when designing the offering strategy, defined in Table 5.1 below.

Table 5.1: Offering Strategy Combinations

Offering Strategy	Example
Same core product with varying service levels	A diagnostics company launches a new digital pathology solution. As part of the offering, the company offers three service levels. Basic, advanced, and gold service.
Different core products with same service levels	A manufacturer of cardiac stents offers two types of cardiac stents. Bare metal stents and drug-eluting stents. The basic service is the same regardless of the type of stent.
Vary both core product and service	A medical imaging company sells two lines of CT scanners as well as offers three different service levels to choose from.

One additional way to vary the offering to improve profitability and provide negotiation flexibility is to look at the business terms that are offered. Business terms govern how you and the customer will do business together. These can often have a significant impact on customer profitability. It is another area that should be connected with the offering strategy. Examples of business terms include:

- Payment terms
- Financing
- Contract length
- Cancellation fees
- Purchase commitments
- Bundles purchased
- Legal terms

In total, there are three broad levers that can be used to adapt the offering. These are the core product, services, and the business terms that surround the deal. These can be visualized in Figure 5.1.

Figure 5.1 – Elements of Offering Strategy

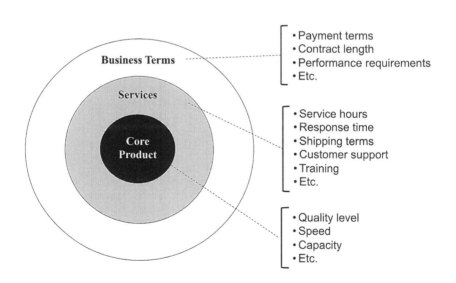

Implementing an Offering Strategy

Giving customers options is a good thing. It has the potential to help the sales team deal with difficult buyers. Options also allow for varying the offering to meet the needs of different buyers. It also affords the company a strategic lever to deal with low-price competitors. Unfortunately, having many options can also result in a mess if the company is not disciplined in its use of the various offerings. So, medical technology companies need to have rules, policies, and controls in implementing an offering strategy.

Rules and policies are simply a means for defining what the offerings are, the prices of the offers, and when the offerings should be used. The offerings also need to be linked to a pricing strategy and price levels. Figure 5.2 shows a simple example of an imaging company selling CT scanners. The way to vary the offering in this example is through the quality and power of various CT scanners offered.

In this example, there are three CT scanners available. A top product offers superior image quality and speed but costs more. A middle product offers a lower cost but also lower image quality. Finally, there is a low-cost product that offers a significant cost savings but has lower image quality. Each of these offerings target a different user type and also have a wide range of cost to serve. They also should have a different price level since they provide very different value to the customer.

Figure 5.2 – Varying Offering Strategy

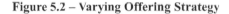

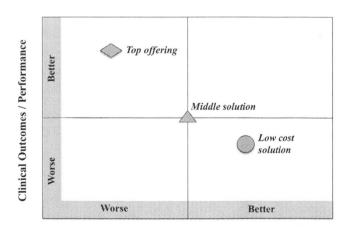

example, different buyers could have varying needs and willing-ness to pay. A privately owned imaging center that targets non-emergency radiology patients may only need a certain quality and speed level. This is also likely to be a more price-sensitive customer since it is privately owned. On the other hand, a large academic medical center with a very busy emergency room may need a high-end CT scanner that is available at all times. This is also likely to be a segment that is relatively less price sensitive compared to the privately owned imaging center. In this example, the top of the line offering is best.

Now consider an example of a company selling a new type of patient-monitoring equipment that has one capital component and a standard service contract that covers Monday through Saturday business hours. In this case, the company has little offering flexibility to deal with customers with varying needs or willingness to pay. The company may encounter a small customer who is not willing to pay the cost for the six-day-a-week service. In order to win the business without a way to adapt the offering, the company would need to discount the core offering beyond where the company may like to discount.

The discounting to win the deal often leads to a lack of price discipline. In the example above, discounting to win business at the smaller customer potentially sets up an issue. What would happen if a large customer with a higher price acquired the smaller customer? Of course the larger customer would be upset and would want a better price. So it should be clear. Without other parts of the offering to adjust, price becomes the means to win the business. This can lead to marginally profitable or unprofitable customers as well as undisciplined pricing.

Managing Customer Profitability

In any marketplace, there are customers of varying size, needs, behaviors, willingness to pay, cost to serve, and ability to negotiate. Approaching these different types of customers with the same essential offering can create issues. If companies are not careful, they can find themselves in a situation where most of the profit is earned by a small percentage of customers.

This means a large percentage of customers are marginally profitable or unprofitable.

A simple chart of cumulative customer profitability will illustrate this situation. This chart, sometime known as the whale curve because of its shape, shows customer profitability. On the vertical axis is cumulative customer profitability. The horizontal axis is customers ranked from most profitable to least profitable. It is often the case that a portion of the customers make up over 100 percent of the profits a company earns. This means that the company is losing money on some segment of customers. This can be seen in Figure 5.3.

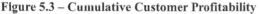

Figure 5.3 – Cumulative Customer Profitability

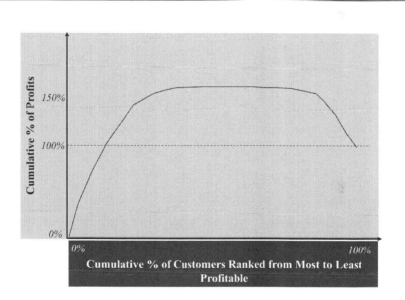

Drivers of Customer Profitability

Part of managing customer profitability is understanding the drivers of customer profitably. Figure 5.4 provides a framework for thinking about customer profitability. There are two main drivers—revenue quality and cost to serve.

Figure 5.4 – Customer Profitability Drivers

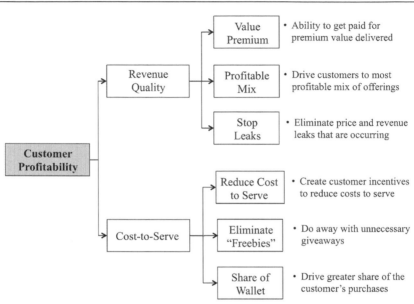

Under the two main drivers are six broad factors that drive customer profitability. These are meant to be generic factors but can be adapted for your business. The factors include:

- *Value premium*: This represents the ability of your company to set prices to capture the portion of premium value you create for customers. Does your pricing recognize that different segments have differing price sensitivity and willingness to pay? Are you earning a price premium where you should? Is your price premium aligned with your cost to serve?

- *Profitable mix*: In many businesses, it is typical that different products and product lines have varying profitability. Therefore, there is an opportunity to set prices and manage revenue to drive customers to more profitable product mix.

- *Stop leaks*: Price and revenue leaks can occur in a number of ways. Contract compliance is an area in medical technology businesses where revenue leaks occur. This is when the customer signs a performance-based contract to earn a discount, but the company does not monitor or enforce the contract. Other price leaks include not charging for service visits, poor price controls in granting of customer discounts, and not charging for services that are typically charged for in your industry.

- *Reduce costs to serve*: Different customers have varying needs, operating characteristics, and behaviors. Often, some small segments of customers over-consume company resources in training, support, and other activities. Therefore, it is important to understand and manage the cost to serve for different customer segments.

- *Eliminate freebies*: Companies sometimes fall into the trap of developing new value-added services and giving freebies to customers in order to compete. Over time, these freebies can end up costing the company lots of money because either there are no rules around which customers have access to freebies or the rules are not followed. These can often be viewed as standard "deal closers" by sales and evolve into table stakes.

- *Share of wallet*: Share of wallet is meant to be a measure of the percentage of the customer's available business you have under contract. It is an important metric from a cost-to-serve perspective. Since a number of the cost-to-serve elements are relatively fixed, a great share of customer's wallet means that the average cost to serve per revenue dollar decreases.

If one of the goals of the business is to earn a profit, then having a clear offering strategy is often a key component of earning a profit. This is particularly true for companies that compete in markets that are in the mature or declining phase of the technology life cycle. It is at this stage of the market life cycle that being able to vary the offering to address the different needs, behaviors, and willingness to pay becomes more important.

Without a clear offering strategy, companies may find themselves in a situation where they are unable to deal with price buyers. They can also find themselves in a situation where they cannot effectively compete with a price competitor. This can lead to losing money on certain customers by over-serving them or over-discounting. Therefore, companies need clarity about what offering should target each buyer type and segment. This will provide negotiation flexibility as well as better align cost to serve with prices.

There is another reason why medical technology companies often need an offering strategy. This has to do with operating in a global environment. The willingness to pay for a medical technology often varies widely across different countries. For example, the willingness to pay for a new cardiovascular technology will be different in the US compared with Greece or India. Therefore, companies need to think through the issues that arise when the same product is sold at varying price levels across the globe. One way to deal with the issue of international med tech pricing is to have a product line or offering strategy. The global pricing dilemma will be fully addressed in chapter eleven.

Conclusion

Having a clear offering strategy is often critical. The need for flexibility in the offering usually increases as the core technology enters the mature and decline phases of the technology life cycle. This is when competition increases and buyers become more able to take risks in purchasing. A flexible offering strategy provides sales negotiation flexibility to deal with difficult buyers. It also provides a strategic lever to deal with price-based competitors while serving different segments of the market. Offering strategies should be developed on purpose, not just evolve over time. Companies without a purposeful approach and clear rules and policies can easily create a messy situation. This can lead to marginal or unprofitable customers, which takes a lot of time, energy, and resolve to clean up.

CHAPTER 6

MEDICAL TECHNOLOGY CONTRACTING AND TENDERING STRATEGY

Contracting and tendering is the means by which the company implements the pricing and offering strategy. Unfortunately, personal experience suggests that it is often confused with the pricing or offering strategy. Companies that have no clear pricing or offering strategy decide on one by default when they enter into contracts or tenders.

Therefore, a critical input to the contracting and tendering strategy should be the pricing and offering strategy. This defines the offerings, the prices for those offerings, the targets for the offerings, and how to fence the prices across segments. Without this clearly defined in advance, the company runs the risk of making many mistakes that could impact growth and profits.

This chapter provides a review of some of the basics of contracting and tendering. It assumes that the company has developed a clear pricing and offering strategy. Contracting and tendering by itself is a very important area and has many nuances that need to be understood and carefully considered. It is also an area where many price and value leaks can occur.

Overview of Contracts and Tenders

Contracts and tenders are the agreements that define the business and legal terms governing the sale/procurement of goods and services. The business terms include the offerings, prices, payment terms, service, and performance requirements of both the buyer and seller. Most, but not all, purchasing transactions in medical technology involve contracts or tenders.

Tenders, in most situations in medical technology, refer to procurement of goods and services by a public entity. These public entities, such as hospitals or laboratories, have specific rules to follow regarding the structure and process for issuing and awarding tenders. For example, in the European Union (EU), there are public tender rules that govern what needs to be on the tender, the process to follow, and how final bids are awarded. Many countries around the world that have publicly financed healthcare have specific rules to follow in the procurement process. In most circumstances, these rules are in place to ensure a fair and open bidding process.

There are many variations to the type of tenders and the specific rules that are followed in awarding bids. There are also sometimes rules around the fair exchange of information during the tendering process and the undue influence of tender requirements. Clever medical technology companies work in advance to shape the tender so that the requirements recognize the unique value that the company can bring. This, of course, has to be done within the specific rules and laws of the country or entity issuing the tender.

Major Contracting Entities

In many markets, the med tech marketer will need to carefully consider the structure of the marketplace and how end users can access contract pricing and terms. In the US, for example, an acute care hospital may have many different ways to access contract pricing and terms for a product. The hospital may belong to two different group purchasing organizations. The hospital could also be part of an integrated delivery network. Finally, the facility can also negotiate its own contracts for supply items. In this case, the hospital has four potential contracts to choose from.

Without an overall pricing strategy, discounting rules, and a thoughtful approach to contracting, the med tech company can run into many problems. The healthcare market is ever changing. There is a constant consolidation of customers. Also, new alliances and business models are emerging. This means there has to be logic in the pricing and contracting approach.

While not an exhaustive list, here is a summary of eleven key types of customer entities that a med tech company could be contracting with. Understanding each entity, its ability to drive market share, and how it could be connected to other entities is important.

- *Physician offices and clinics:* This category includes solo physician practices and physician group practices that purchases medical supplies and services.

- *Distributors:* There are many types of distributors. This category is referring to distributors who take title to the goods, and then resell the goods to the end users. Distributors are the main means to supply certain segments of customers or are the main means to sell in certain countries.

- *Standalone hospital or surgical center:* These are acute hospitals or surgical centers that operate independently and do not belong to a hospital chain or integrated delivery network. These are short-term stay, acute care facilities. These entities can contract directly with the med tech company or purchase off of GPO contracts.

- *Integrated delivery network (IDN):* These are groups of acute care hospitals, surgical centers, clinics, laboratories, and physician offices that are members of a separate parent legal entity. They often contract as a group with med tech suppliers. These IDNs take on many different forms, and their ability to control the IDN members' purchasing varies widely.

113

- *Hospital chains:* These are for-profit or not-for-profit acute care hospital chains that own and operate many hospitals. They can be members of a GPO. These entities stereotypically have much greater control and ability to drive supply purchasing across member hospitals.

- *Group purchasing organizations (GPOs):* GPOs are a form of a buying group where hundreds or thousands of hospitals aggregate their purchasing volume to contract with med tech and pharmaceutical companies. Hospitals are members of the buying group and can also be shareholders in the GPO. GPOs will be discussed in greater detail in the next chapter.

- *National or international reference labs:* These are large national or international for-profit chains of clinical laboratories. They usually have significant ability to drive compliance to the terms of the supply agreements.

- *Regional reference labs:* These are regionally based clinical laboratories. These entities operate within a region of a country. They normally have significant control over purchasing and can drive compliance to the terms of the agreement.

- *Imaging-center chains:* Imaging-center chains are multi-facility imaging entities that own, manage, or lease more than one diagnostic imaging center. The imaging center typically has multiple imaging modalities.

- *Single-site imaging center:* This is a single standalone diagnostic imaging center.

- *Government:* These are government institutions, regional buying authorities, and other government entities who procure goods and services.

Contact Types and Structure

While all of the different combinations of contracting types and structure can seem confusing, there are some very basic elements that make up most contracts. The med tech company will need to think about the contract structure and types in the context of an overall offering strategy (this was discussed in chapter five). This will help to provide negotiation flexibility when dealing with different buyer types.

The first element to consider is the type of contract. Type refers to the supplier's position on the contract. There are three basic types:

- *Sole-source contract:* This contract simply means that the supplier and customer have agreed that the supplier will be the sole supplier for the supply items under contract. In practice, this usually means the customer agrees to purchase 90 percent or more of a given category or item from the supplier. The customer has the advantage of standardizing on one supplier for better terms. The supplier has the advantage of reducing average cost to serve.

- *Dual-source contact:* In this contract, the customer agrees to only source a certain supply item or category from two suppliers. Often, market-share commitments are set at or around 50 percent. A dual-source arrangement allows the customer to negotiate better terms and still provides some choice or flexibility to end users.

- *Multi-source contracts:* In this arrangement, more than two suppliers are chosen to be on contract. This essentially provides the supplier an opening in the account, but usually no purchase commitments from the customer. The pricing is usually less favorable for the customer.

The next element to consider is the contract structure. The contract structure has a number of components that can help shape customer behavior and impact the profitability of the deal to the supplier. These components can also be used as trade-offs during the negotiation process. A summary of the components is as follows:

- *Discounts:* This is the level of discount the customer can earn based on objective criteria such as volume purchased, market share, or contract type. The customer begins earning the discount with each purchase. Customers favor the approach because they receive the discount as part of the normal purchase. Suppliers dislike this because usually the discount is an earned discount based on performance, and performance is measured retrospectively. This means if the customer doesn't meet a volume or market-share goal, it is hard to get back discounts that the customer has already received.

- *Performance rebate:* This is a payment after the fact based on the customer meeting some objective performance criteria. The criteria could be elements like market share, volume purchases, or new product adoption. For example, a supplier could set a growth rebate that rewards the customer with an annual rebate of 5 percent of incremental annual sales over the prior year.

- *Price protection or price increases:* This defines the amount of annual price increase the supplier is able to take as part of the agreement.

- *Contract length:* This is simply the term of the agreement. Usually, suppliers can ask for a longer agreement when pressed for better pricing. This is one of the trades that can be made during negotiations.

- *Payment terms:* This is the period of time that the customer has to pay. Given the global financial crisis and the government debt levels around the world, this is becoming an increasingly important component to focus on in the contract.

- *Financing method:* For med tech businesses with capital equipment as part of the offering, whether the customer rents, purchases, or leases, the capital can play a role in the pricing and terms of the deal.

- *Contract compliance terms:* Contract compliance refers to the timing and process for the supplier and customer to agree on whether or not the customer is performing up to the terms of the agreement. Often, companies grant upfront discounts for products based on a customer commitment to a certain purchase volume or market share. The supplier needs a process to check that the customer is meeting the terms of the agreement. This should be one of the components of the contract.

- *Most-favored-nations clause:* This clause provides that if you offer better pricing to another customer, the "favored" customer shall be entitled to the pricing. In practice, this is difficult to manage and track since price is one single element of the deal and is often dependent on many other components. Also, in the US, this could have implications for government contracting.

- *Billing method:* Some med tech sectors have different ways to bill customers for the use of the product. Most of the time, customers are billed based on units or packages purchased. However, some med tech companies bill based on procedure. Other times, in diagnostics for example, customers can be billed based on the number of patient results reported.

Discount Strategy for Medical Technologies

It is usually through the contracting process that the discount strategy is implemented. The discounting strategy is simply deciding how customers can earn a discount. By developing a clear pricing strategy and offering strategy, the company should already have a good idea of the:

- Target segments
- Offerings for each target segment
- Target price level for each segment and a basic price structure (list price, target price, and floor price)
- Price fences to use to fence off each segment
- Price metrics

The company still needs to decide on the discounting strategy. The discounting strategy is going to vary based on each unique situation. For example, a company may be selling a product to a very narrow segment and decide that it only needs to offer nominal discounts as a means to allow customers to negotiate. After all, many customers have been conditioned to negotiate for better pricing. This is particularly true in the age of professional procurement and materials management.

On the other hand, the company may be selling the same product to various segments with a wide variation in value, significant differences in purchasing volume, and big differences in cost to serve. In this case, the company will need a clear discounting strategy that helps align those factors. In general, the discounting strategy needs to consider:

- *Value and willingness to pay:* A product or offering can have a wide variation in value and willingness to pay across the target segments. The company needs to ensure that the discounting provides flexibility to meet the value needs of target segments while still earning a reasonable return.

- *Cost to serve*: The variations in cost to serve across customers and segments will drive the amount of discounts. Ideally, the company needs to align discounting in a way to create incentives for the customer to reduce the company's cost to serve.

- *Purchasing volume or value*: Customers who purchase significantly more volume than other customers will naturally want better pricing. In most markets, customers have been conditioned to expect better discounts the greater the purchasing volume.

- *Related purchases*: Customers who purchase a broader range of products or services from a supplier may expect better pricing. In addition, these customers often, all things being equal, will have a lower average cost to serve. The amount of related purchases by the customer may be a factor to consider in the discounting strategy.

- *Share of wallet*: Customers who purchase a greater share of a particular category of spending from the supplier should receive better pricing. The average cost to serve per unit usually declines for the supplier as some of the fixed elements of cost to serve are spread over more sales.

- *Contract type*: The type of contract should drive the level of discounting. A sole-source contract should receive better pricing than a dual-source contract, all things being equal.

- *Ability to drive performance*: Some larger customers who own, manage, or lease multiple facilities have a variation in their ability to standardize purchases across all facilities. Some larger customers are easily able to standardize purchasing across multiple facilities for many supply items. Other larger customers lack the ability to control buying decisions at the individual facilities. The ability to drive compliance to the performance terms of the agreement should be considered in the discounting strategy.

Force-rank Customers to Drive Discounting Logic and Make Choices

In the end, within a given market, the discounting strategy needs to be logical, defendable, aligned with cost to serve, and able to drive the right customer behaviors. In some markets and situations, it is helpful to force-rank key customers and segments. This helps to make sure the organization is aligned on the relative attractiveness of each customer and segment. This also helps in understanding where the discount dollars will be allocated so that the company can achieve its price level targets.

The goal of this exercise would not be to lay out all six thousand acute care hospitals in the US as an example. Rather, the goal should be to broadly understand which large IDNs, hospital chains, GPOs, and segments fall in relative priority. Often, the organization has differing opinions and perspectives on which IDN, GPO, or key customers should qualify for a level of discounting. Rather than decide on an ad-hoc basis, it would be helpful to be proactive and make choices strategically.

Figure 6.1 shows a map of discount prioritization. In this example, there are four factors or criteria that drive discount prioritization. The factors are purchasing value, ability of customer to control purchasing across its institution or entities, the strategic importance of the segment or customer, and the cost to serve. For each factor, a weighting is used. Each major customer or segment is scored on a scale of one to ten on each factor. The customer score on each factor is multiplied by the factor weighting to arrive at a total point score for the customer or segment. For example, if the company rated Hospital Chain 1 as a ten out of ten on points for ability to control purchasing, this would be multiplied by 40 percent to arrive at a score of four points for that factor. The same approach would be taken for the other factors. These would then be added together for a total score for Hospital Chain 1. A basic spreadsheet would facilitate this process.

Figure 6.1 – Customer Discount Prioritization

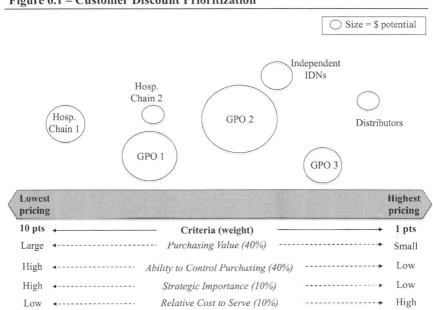

With a rough prioritization in hand, the organization can then have a discussion and get aligned on the results. This helps to make the prioritization of accounts, segments, and channels explicit and clear. It also helps to highlight differences in assumptions about each of the segments or customers. The criteria or factors in Figure 6.1 are examples. These may or may not apply to your business and market. As part of this process, the organization will want to agree on the factors that are important for prioritizing the relative discounts that customers should earn.

Some markets, like the US, have multiple buying groups, many hospital chains, and numerous segments. Without some clear logic and prioritization of accounts, the result can be messy, and it can be hard to defend discounts. Since there is a fair amount of price transparency at the buying-group level, any inconsistency in discounting logic will likely be spotted. A discount prioritization like this also has the advantage of getting everyone to tell the same story to customers about how to earn better discounts.

Discount Rules, Policies, and Controls

Discounting rules and policies are one of the mechanisms to control discounting on an operational basis. Every day there are customer tenders and requests for proposals (RFPs) issued. Without a clear set of guidelines, pricing can get out of control quickly. Discount rules and policies describe how discounts will be granted to customers. These should be written documents that are updated as needed to reflect the agreed upon pricing, offering, and discounting strategy. Without clear discount rules and policies, all of the company's efforts at developing good pricing strategy and quantifying value can go to waste.

Discount controls are the other mechanism used to ensure that discounts are granted in accordance with the pricing and offering strategy. The controls are often described as an approval or escalation process for exceptions. In many markets, there may be situations where it makes sense for the company to make exceptions to the discount rules and policies. It could be due to a special circumstance or an event not fully thought about in the existing discounting rules and policies. The discount controls describe who in the organization has what level of authority in making pricing and terms exception decisions. Discount controls should also include standard financial reporting and analytics on discount trends, price exceptions, and price realization.

Without clear discount rules, policies, and controls, the company's pricing can end up in a mess. Usually, one of the basic criteria that many companies use to grant discounts is volume of purchases. Customers who buy more receive better pricing than customers who buy less. The easiest way to check for issues in discounting rules, policies, and controls is to develop a simple scatter plot. On the vertical axis is price, and on the horizontal axis is volume. Each dot represents a customer.

If there are good policies, rules, and controls in place, you would expect to see a correlation, as shown in the shaded section of Figure 6.2. Unfortunately, the actual price points often look like a shotgun blast, as shown in Figure 6.2. There could be a number of potential causes for this. First, the company could be making discounting decisions based on factors in addition to volume level. These factors are not be reflected in the chart, and therefore it appears as though there are not good controls in place. On the other hand, it could simply be that the company does not have good policies, rules, or controls in place for granting discounts.

Figure 6.2 – Scatter Plot of Discounts

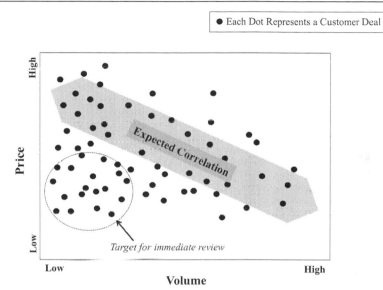

If the shotgun blast is the result of poor policies, rules, and controls, then the issue becomes what to do with a situation like the one shown in Figure 6.2. There is often concern in the organization about adjusting existing customers' prices for fear of losing the customer. Going back to the discussion of customer profitability in chapter five, this chart will help to highlight potential customers who are unprofitable or marginally profitable.

The customers who are circled are smaller customers who have low prices. These customers are often the ones who are candidates for a deeper dive on customer profitability. If it turns out that these customers are unprofitable for the company, then the company has some simple choices. Either increase pricing, fire the customers, or lose money and create the risk that some large customer will ultimately find out that this much smaller customer has better pricing.

Where Do Price Leaks Occur?

The contracting area can be ripe for price leaks. Since contracting is where the implementation of price strategy meets the customer, it is an area where the pressure to win business can often drive poor pricing. In the heat of customer negotiations, decisions can be made that are later regretted. Also, poor process can lead to leaks. Here is a summary of the areas in the contracting process with the biggest leaks:

- *Contract compliance:* Suppliers sign performance-based agreements with customers and do not have a process to track compliance. This means the customer earns discounts that it is not entitled to earn. Once the customer uses the product, it is usually very difficult to go and ask for more money or to bill the customer for under-purchasing against commitments.

- *Price increases:* Companies often go through the process of negotiating annual price increases into agreements. However, many times they lack a process or the will to take an annual price increase.

- *Discounts:* Lack of discounting rules and controls is usually an area of price leak. This simply means that there are not clear discounting rules and policies or that these rules and policies are not followed in practice.

- *Cherry picking:* In markets where the customer has multiple potential contracts to buy off of, a company without clear logic in discounts across contracts can have a significant issue. This is when the customer "cherry picks" pricing from the best contract available.

- *Free services and extras:* Sometimes free services are routinely included in the deal regardless of the level of price negotiated. Or, worse yet, the sales organization becomes conditioned to throw in free service or extras to close the deal. When this becomes a habit, company profitability is sure to suffer.

Conclusion

Contracting is an extremely important area in med tech pricing. This is where the pricing strategy meets the customer. Med tech suppliers need to understand the customers with whom they are contracting. This knowledge includes how all the various entities are related and the relative control each entity has on the purchase decision. Med tech suppliers also need a clear understanding of the pricing structure and type of contracts to drive the right customer behavior and the firm's profitability.

CHAPTER 7

COMMUNICATING AND SELLING VALUE OF MEDICAL TECHNOLOGIES

Setting prices based on value is a good first step. However, without appropriate value communication to convince providers and payers of the value of a product or solution, the med tech firm will struggle to achieve the value-based price. This chapter is focused on value communication. This includes developing a communication strategy, understanding the type of value communication tools available, and implementing value selling in the sales organization.

Value is something perceived by the customer. A company can have an exceptional product or solution, but without the right messaging, tools, and evidence, the customer is often unlikely to know or recognize the value. Unless the customer can observe the benefits firsthand, the company needs to communicate the value to shape the customers' value perceptions. There are a number of important points regarding value and communication to consider:

- Value is perceived, thus implying the seller can influence the buyer's perception of value through effective communication.
- Value is expressed in monetary and clinical terms and is what the customer receives in exchange for the price paid. This

means that raising or lowering the price of the offering does not change its value. Changing the price only changes the buyer's incentive to purchase (1).

- At a given price, all things being equal, a seller who excels at value communication could potentially sell more compared with a seller who does a poor job of value communication.

- Finally, value is relative to competing alternatives and prices. For buyer firms, an alternative could be the status quo.

One of the pricing and marketing goals of the medical technology company should be to gain a clear understanding of the actual value of the technology or offering. The actual value is the quantifiable economic and clinical value. With this in hand, the company then can use these value insights to shape the customers' perceptions of value through an effective value communication strategy. Without an understanding of value, it's hard to effectively influence other's value perceptions.

Value Communication Strategy

A well-thought-out communication strategy should include choices such as:

- Objectives of the communication
- Target audience
- Key messages
- Communication tools to use
- Communication frequency
- Communication intensity
- Economics of the proposed communication strategy

In business-to-business markets, there are a number of marketing communication channels that firms can use to reach target audiences, such as advertising, sales promotions, public relations and publicity, direct marketing, and personal selling (2). In the med tech markets, personal selling, key opinion leaders, scientific meetings, and clinical publications are important communication channels to inform target audiences of the clinical and economic benefits.

In communicating value, the marketer will need to decide what benefits to communicate and which audience to target. In a buyer organization, there are different stakeholders involved in the purchase and supplier selection decision. These include the user buyer, the technical buyer, and the economic buyer (3). These buyers can be individuals or groups of people.

For example, a value analysis committee in a hospital acts as a buying center. The value analysis committee is classically comprised of representatives from the clinical department, physicians, materials management, and others in hospital administration. As in any buying center, each member of the group has a set of individual preferences and a range of influence on the buying decision (4).

In med tech, there is the additional hurdle of often needing to convince the payer the product is a good value for money. Therefore, in addition to the typical buying influences at a provider, there is also the payer to influence. Figure 7.1 provides a summary of the intersection of the target audiences and the benefits communicated.

Figure 7.1 – Benefit Communication Matrix

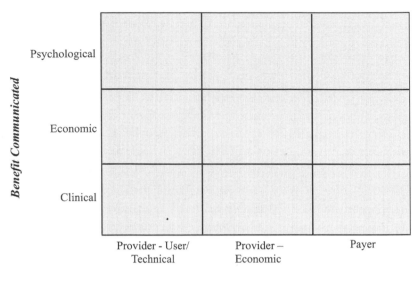

After deciding on the objectives of the value communication strategy, the communication strategy should then address who needs to be targeted (audience) and what benefit messages would be most impactful (benefit type). Figure 7.1 provides a useful framework for planning the communication. It should be clear after completing the framework if there are gaps in the communication strategy.

It is often the case that medical technologies have some form of clinical evidence and messaging available. After all, clinical data is required to gain regulatory approval. However, there are sometimes issues with the depth, breadth, and quality of evidence to satisfy all target audiences. Moreover, there are often issues with the quality or availability of economic evidence and tools available to support value communications. The next section will deal specifically with economic value communication tools.

Economic Value Communication Tools

Since pricing is most directly tied to the economic value, the focus here will be on economic value communication. This is not to say that the other elements of value are not important. On the contrary, these other elements of value communication are extremely important. The focus on economic is because many med tech firms struggle with economic value communication.

Given the rising importance of the economic buyer in the purchasing process, sellers will need to decide what economic benefits to communicate and how to communicate those benefits. There are a range of tools and tactics available to communicate economic benefits. These vary from relatively simple to highly complex tools and tactics. Often, sellers use a variety of these tools in combination to target buyers along the consumer response stages. These stages include awareness, interest, evaluation, trial, and adoption (5).

There is no standard definition for the types of economic benefit communication tools in use today. Various terms are used to describe these tools. Based on the author's experience and an evaluation of case examples, definitions were developed. For purposes of this discussion, four categories of economic benefit communication tools will be defined. These include economic benefit claims, decision support analytical models, workflow/business model studies, and guarantees/risk sharing. Each of these will be discussed in detail.

Economic Benefit Claims

First, there are economic benefit claims. Economic benefit claims are statements, messages, and marketing collateral based on some evidence or data regarding the economic benefit of using the supplier's solution. These benefit communications can be delivered through numerous communication channels, including websites, personal selling, peer-reviewed publications, and advertising. These tools include customer self-reported data, observational studies, and prospective studies.

A benefit claim is used to present facts and data and is a non-interactive form of communication. Essentially, it is a one-way communication from the seller to the buyer and is usually intended to establish evidence and credibility regarding the economic impact of the supplier's solution. In choosing this type of communication tool, the seller will need to consider factors such as industry norms, the amount and type of evidence required to positively influence buyers, and the investment required to generate the claims.

For some products and offerings, large-scale prospective economic studies are used to develop economic benefit communications. Consider the case of Cordis, the company that launched the first drug-eluting stent in the world. Drug-eluting stents are tiny metal scaffolds that are inserted into the patient's coronary artery to prop open a blocked artery. The metal scaffolds are coated with a drug that improves the effectiveness of the device. Cordis invested in economic studies across a large number of patients to collect and compare costs of treatment across hundreds of hospitals (6). These types of studies measure the costs and benefits of using the new medical device in a controlled clinical trial, and study results are usually published in peer-reviewed journals.

The next type of economic benefit claims is observational studies. These represent studies based on the supplier observing the impact of its solution on one or more customers in order to understand the costs and benefits. These studies are often referred to as value-in-use studies or single-center studies.

Decision Support Analytical Models

The next category of economic benefit communication tools is decision support analytical models. For purposes of this discussion, a decision analytic model will be defined as a logical mathematical framework that combines inputs, assumptions, and data to help inform buyer decision makers (7). The value of the model lies not only in the results it produces but also in revealing the causal logic between inputs and outputs (8).

From a seller's perspective, the intent is to not only educate and inform but also to persuade the buyer. Unlike economic benefit claims, these tools allow for an interactive exchange. Usually the tools allow the buyer to input operational variables and assumptions in order to understand the range of potential economic benefits.

In practice, these tools have a variety of names. *Value calculator* usually refers to a spreadsheet or other software tool used to evaluate the financial impact of using a solution over a defined period of time. It may be compared to the next best alternative. The value calculator is used to compare the financial impact from a total cost of ownership or total cost impact perspective. Total cost of ownership is meant to capture the costs to acquire, use, maintain, and dispose of a solution. Costs would include all incremental costs of buying and using the solution less all potential cost offsets. The tool may also include the revenue impact as well.

The term *ROI calculator* is often used to refer to a financial model that is used to calculate a return on investment (ROI) over a defined period of time. The model is in a spreadsheet or other software. In this type of modeling, there is usually a one-time investment for start-up or capital costs for the new solution. Therefore, the model compares the initial investment to financial benefits that occur over time in order to calculate a return. The calculations are done from the perspective of the provider or asset owner.

For example, a hospital may be evaluating the investment in RFID (radio frequency identification) technology to track blood donations and blood products. The implementation of the system would require an initial investment in IT infrastructure, software, and training. These would be one-time costs. In addition, the hospital would require ongoing costs in RFID tags, software licenses, and periodic training for new hires.

In implementing the new system and processes, the hospital would gain a number of operational improvements. These benefits would be less waste of costly blood products, fewer potential errors, and less time spent tracking and monitoring inventory. The result of the one-time investments, ongoing savings, and new costs would be used to compute a return on investment along with a payback period in number of years or months (9).

Workflow/Business Model Studies

The next category of economic benefit communication tools is workflow and business model studies. These are before and after studies that are performed by the seller in collaboration with the buyer. These normally occur when the seller is marketing a complete solution or a significant change in how the buyer will operate a major business process. It could also involve a major change to the business model of the buyer's firm. In this case, it is difficult for the buyer to independently evaluate and understand the economic benefits of the seller's solution. Therefore, the seller needs to work collaboratively with the buyer to prepare a clear before-and-after picture of the economic benefits of making a change.

One example is studies that are completed in order to sell hospital laboratory automation solutions. Many hospitals are moving to automating their laboratories for routine blood testing. In the past, hospitals operated numerous different types of instruments that perform blood tests with separate processes. Many of these instruments required hospital personnel to load and remove patient samples. With the advent of laboratory automation, robotics and automation technology is used to eliminate many manual processes such as loading, storing, and moving patient samples. Automation results in less labor costs and also improves quality and provides timelier test results. This often requires a complete redesign of the hospital laboratory. Manufacturers such as Ortho Clinical Diagnostics sell automation equipment along with the service to redesign laboratory processes through lean six sigma (10).

Guarantees/Risk Sharing

The final category of economic benefit communication tools are guarantees and risk-sharing arrangements. A guarantee or risk-sharing arrangement is a form of economic benefit communication where the supplier agrees to take on a portion of the risk of its product or solution achieving a desired outcome. The outcome could be clinical or economic. This is becoming increasingly common in healthcare, where payers and providers struggle with funding all of the new technologies that come to market each year.

Take the example of Genomics Health (GHDX). GHDX is a California-based innovative diagnostics company. Oncotype DX breast cancer assay is a multigene expression test, developed and marketed by GHDX, that physicians currently use to predict the likelihood of chemotherapy benefit and recurrence risk for patients with early-stage, estrogen-receptor-positive breast cancer. Prior to this test being available, doctors relied on treatment guidelines that took into account inputs like the size and type of cancer tumor to decide who should receive chemotherapy (11).

In the traditional diagnostics testing industry, where a fifty-dollar test is considered expensive, GHDX set the price of its new diagnostic test at approximately $3,500. The value proposition to payers (government and private insurers) was simple. Based on existing treatment guidelines, some percentage of patients were receiving expensive chemotherapy (approximately $15,000) that the GHDX test suggested was not necessary. In order to persuade payers that the test was a good value for money, GHDX developed economic studies and value models to prove that if physicians used insights from the new test, the test would be a fair value at $3,500.

However, for some payers, the evidence was not enough. A common challenge in the diagnostics industry is to prove not only that a test provides new clinical insights but also that physicians would use insights from the test to change clinical practice. From a payer perspective, the payer is worse off if it pays for an expensive diagnostic test and the doctors do not follow the test results. So GHDX went a step further. They entered into risk-sharing arrangements, where they tracked, along with a payer, whether the test was having the intended impact on clinical practice. If the number of patients receiving chemotherapy exceeded an agreed-upon threshold, even if the test suggested that the patients would not benefit, the insurer received a pre-negotiated lower price (12). In this example, the supplier used multiple tools/tactics to create an integrated communication strategy including large-scale economic studies, value calculators, and guarantees.

Summary of Economic Benefit Communication Tools

Figure 7.2 shows the various communication tools segmented by communication type and complexity of communication. Communication type refers to whether it is a one-way or two-way communication. The complexity of communication involves the degree of complexity involved in the communication of benefits. Medical technology marketers will need to decide on the appropriate tools for the situation and communication objectives.

Figure 7.2 – Economic Benefit Communication Tools

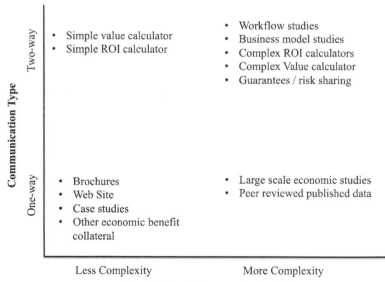

Implementing Value Selling

"All the vendors' solutions are roughly the same; it now comes down to price." For med tech suppliers, hearing this from customers is usually a sign of trouble. It could simply be a negotiation ploy. Often, it is a smart procurement manager who uses a phrase like this to try to set the stage for negotiations. Alternatively, it could be the legitimate perception of the customer, often caused by suppliers confusing customers by focusing on collateral and messaging filled with features and very little value. In either case, for unprepared suppliers, it can result in eroding prices and margins.

The previous sections of the chapter dealt with value communication strategy and the economic value communication tools available. At this point, given that personal selling is a critical communication channel, the focus needs to be on how to operationalize value selling and communications in the sales organization. There are a number of key success factors to making it work. Each will be discussed in detail.

Develop Simple, Honest, and Accurate Communication and Selling Tools

There are a number of important design criteria for creating usable and helpful value selling tools. Some of these are fairly obvious, and some may seem counterintuitive. However, the ability to have the sales organization adopt and readily use value-selling tools comes down to getting these design criteria right.

Table 7.1 provides a six-sigma view, called a critical-to-quality tree, of these design criteria. A critical-to-quality (CTQ) tree is a simple tool that helps translate customer language into quantified requirements for product/service design. In this instance, both sales representatives and the end customers were viewed as the "customer" in order to delineate the design criteria for selling tools.

Table 7.1 – Value Selling Tool CTQ Tree

Need (high-level)	Drivers	Critical-to-Quality (CTQs) (specific and measurable)
Simple	Easy to use	• Takes sales rep less than a half hour to complete tool for a customer • Average sales representative can use without issues
	Easy to learn	• Can use distance learning to teach tool to sales representative • Training required is less than one hour
	Easy to understand	• Average sales representative can easily understand • Output is clear and understandable for 90 percent or more customers • Critical few value drivers that make up majority of value are identified (80/20)
Believable	Accurate	• Calculations are accurate • Eighty percent or more of value difference is quantified • Tool reflects current competitive alternatives
	Honest	• Show both positive and negative value
	Evidence based	• Assumptions and calculations supported by studies or data • Sources of data clearly documented
	Transparent	• Benefit logic and formulas are clearly stated
Customizable	Customer specific	• Uses customer-specific data to create customized value analysis
Integrated	Supports selling process	• Language in tool supports selling process • Not seen as extra work by sales representatives

In the CTQ tree in Table 7.1, each high-level need is ultimately translated into very specific and measurable design criteria. For example, the need to have a selling tool that is believable is ultimately translated into seven very specific and measurable criteria. Whether the tool that is being used to communicate value is a Web-based value model or a spreadsheet-based selling tool, it is important to try to follow these basic design principles. Depending on the industry characteristics and norms, there may be other CTQs to consider. However, this should be a reasonable list to start with.

Support Tools with Evidence

Having a simple value calculator or ROI tool is necessary but not sufficient. While some customers may not challenge the assumptions and calculations, many customers will. In addition, for many medical technologies, legal and regulatory requirements will dictate the need for evidence. In most cases, the company has to be careful that any value communication is supported by appropriate evidence and is consistent with regulatory approvals.

Obviously, the level of evidence required will vary depending on things like industry practices, the size of customer expenditure, the risk involved in the purchase decision, and how much of the value created is to be captured. For example, the level of evidence required for a major new medical device that could be used in millions of patients with cardiovascular disease may be very different than the evidence needed for a hospital software solution to improve storage of medical images.

Integrate Tools into Selling Process

Depending on the structure of your business and the industry selling practices, there may be a variety of groups involved in communicating value to customers. These groups can range from key account executives to sales representatives to field-based marketing people to reimbursement managers. In practice, within any of these groups, there are probably individuals who are doing an outstanding job of communicating value today. Often, these are the same individuals who may have already created their own "home-brew" value-selling tools. An important part of the buy-in and change process will be to identify and involve these individuals in the efforts.

From experience, these talented sales professionals usually develop their own value-selling tools for a couple of reasons:

- Existing value-selling tools are inadequate. The tools provided by the marketing groups are too complicated, not compelling, or not working for some reason.
- No tools are provided. Savvy sales personnel have given up the feature-laden brochures and have figured out the few critical value messages to communicate to customers.

Involving field thought leaders has a number of benefits. First, existing good work that has already been developed can be leveraged. This will speed up the efforts. Second, from a change management perspective, getting key thought leaders and respected people from the sales organization on board will help gain broader buy-in from the sales organization.

Another important point is to assess and identify the critical training required for the field at large to be able to use value-selling tools successfully. In most organizations, there is a wide variation in skills, knowledge, and strengths. Often, the sales organization will need to be trained not just on what value is and how to use the tools, but they will also need to be educated on how to speak the financial language of customers. Finally, they should be armed with objection-handling tools and critical messages to go along with the selling effort. Without a well-prepared and bought-in field sales organization, any effort to implement value selling will not likely see significant benefits.

One critical part of implementing value-selling tools is being able to integrate these into the overall sales process. Unfortunately, many businesses lack a formal or well-defined sales process. A recent survey of businesses of all sizes indicated that only 43 percent have a well-defined sales process (13). For businesses that have a well-defined process, integrating value-selling tools should be relatively easy. Integrating into the sales process will require getting field sales input on how and when to use the tools as part of the normal process. Pilots should also be considered to test the new tools as part of the sales process.

For businesses without a formally defined sales process, implementing value-selling tools could prove very difficult. While a segment of sales representatives will naturally use the tools, getting the majority of the organization on board will be a challenge. For businesses that are in this situation, the right starting point may be to develop a basic sales process first and then move to value selling. It usually will prove difficult to gain widespread usage and adoption without a clear selling process in place.

Build Marketing Capability and Leadership Support

The ability of the organization to develop, maintain, and update value-selling tools is usually reliant on marketing. The marketing organization needs to build the skills, expertise, and processes to ensure that the tools remain updated and usable by sales. Often, one of the root causes of tools not being used is the fact that they can become outdated, and sales will stop using them.

In addition, the support of sales and marketing leadership is critical for value selling to be effective. Marketing needs to execute an overall communication strategy and evidence development. Sales needs to build the skills and processes to effectively communicate value. Lastly, senior management needs to provide the funding, resources, and direction to make value selling a strategic capability for the firm.

Conclusion

In med tech markets, value is perceived. It represents a combination of the economic, clinical, and psychological benefits received in exchange for the price paid, relative to alternative solutions. This means that sellers have the opportunity to shape buyers' value perceptions. Many providers and payers, even sophisticated ones, lack the tools or data necessary to assess the economic benefits of suppliers' solutions. So, what do they know?

Being rational buyers, many economic buyers at least know and can evaluate one dimension of the offering. This, of course, is the price of the offering compared to other alternatives. In the absence of clear and convincing economic benefit communication, the seller risks losing a buyer who is focused primarily on price. This can lead to price competition and erosion.

One way to combat this price competition and erosion is to develop an integrated economic value communication strategy. This is not about simply developing a value calculator and handing it to the sales force. It is about developing a comprehensive communication strategy and the right messages and communication tools to successfully defend value.

NOTES

1. Anderson, J., Thomson, J., Wynstra, F., (2000) Combining value and price to make purchase decisions in business markets, International Journal of Research in Marketing, Volume 17, Issue 4, Pages 307-329

2. Kotler (2003) A Framework for marketing management (2nd ed.): Prentice-Hall. Upper Saddle River, NJ

3. Miller, R., and Heiman, S., (1986) Strategic Selling. Warner Books Inc. New York, NY.

4. Perdue B., Summers J., (1991) Purchasing Agents' Use of Negotiation Strategies. Journal of Marketing Research. May. 28(2): 175-189.

5. Rodgers, E., (1995) Diffusion of Innovation. (4th ed.): The Free Press New York, NY.

6. Ryan J, and Cohen DJ., (2006) Are drug-eluting stents cost-effective? It depends on whom you ask. Circulation. 114: 1736-44.

7. Weinstein, M., O'Brien, B., Hornberg, J., Jackson, J., Johannesson, M., McCabe, C., Luce, B., (2003). Principles of Good Practice for Decision Analytic Modeling in Health-Care Evaluation: Report of The ISPOR Task Force on Good Research Practices - Modeling Studies. Value in Health. Vol. 6.

8. IBID

9. This example was adapted from: http://transfusionmedicinerfid.org/financial-roi-modelhospital.html

10. See www.orthoclinical.com

11. Carlson, J., Garrison, L., and Sullivan, S. (2009) Paying for Outcomes: Innovative Coverage and Reimbursement Schemes for Pharmaceuticals. Journal of Managed Care Pharmacy. October, 2009

12. IBID

13. Accenture. (2010) Optimizing Sales Effectiveness to Achieve High Performance. accessed December 18, 2010

PART III

SPECIAL MEDICAL TECHNOLOGY
PRICING TOPICS

CHAPTER 8

ROLE OF REIMBURSEMENT AND EVIDENCE

Reimbursement is a critical area when it comes to pricing. Reimbursement policy and payment levels can impact price sensitivity for medical technologies. Likewise, price levels can influence the reimbursement that a technology receives. It can be a very complicated area with differing rules for inpatient care, outpatient care, and diagnostic services.

There are also varying rules, policies, and payment mechanisms across the globe. So, for the average decision maker trying to make a pricing or commercial decision based on an understanding of reimbursement, it can be extremely difficult. This chapter provides perspective on the role of reimbursement in pricing decisions for medical technologies.

Most countries around the world face the daunting challenge of funding high-quality healthcare for their citizens. This involves making choices on what health services and technologies represent good value for money. This funding challenge is growing ever more difficult due to demographic trends, the global economy, and the pace of technology innovation. It is up to the medical technology company to understand the system in order to get a fair value for the technology they provide but not to take unfair advantage of the system.

147

Types of Reimbursement Systems

Reimbursement is referred to in many ways. For purposes of this book, reimbursement is defined as payment to a caregiver or asset owner by a payer or patient for healthcare services provided. A caregiver could be a physician, nurse, therapist, or other person involved in patient care. An asset owner is the person or organization who owns the assets where care is provided and can include hospitals, outpatient centers, doctors' offices, laboratories, and others. Depending on where in the world the care is provided, payment to the caregiver and asset owner can take a variety of forms.

There are a number of basic reimbursement systems operating today around the world for medical technologies and medical services. The basic types of systems include capitated payments, fee for service, global budgets, per diems, and patient pay. Payment can vary based on where the medical technology is used, who uses it, and how it is used. This chapter will present the basic systems, but realize that there are variants.

Capitated Payments

Capitated payment systems are reimbursement mechanisms where the caregiver or asset owner is reimbursed one fixed amount for the episode of care. For example, in the US, Medicare reimburses hospitals based on a diagnosis-related group (DRG) for inpatient care. This is a prospective payment system that covers all the costs of care excluding physician fees. In this system, all patients who are given care in the inpatient setting fall into one of roughly 750 DRGs. The number of DRGs changes over time as procedures change, new technologies are introduced, and the system undergoes further refinements.

Each DRG has its own payment amount. The payment is determined through a complicated cost-based method and basically represents an average cost. Hospitals, therefore, have an incentive to reduce their costs below the "average" DRG payment to earn a profit. Many other developed countries like Germany and France have some form of a DRG system.

Fee for Service

Fee for service is a payment mechanism where the payer pays the hospital or physician a fixed amount for providing a service. For example, as part of a routine physical, a physician may order laboratory tests for a patient. In a fee-for-service environment, the laboratory would bill the payer for the lab tests that are performed. Much of physician reimbursement in the US for services provided is based on a fee-for-service payment mechanism.

Global Budgets

In some countries, the reimbursement system works on the basis of a global budget. In the simple form, the government provides a fixed "global budget" to the hospital or region to care for all patients in a given region. This budget then must be allocated by the hospital or region to pay for all of the services provided. The hospital has the responsibility for determining what services it will offer.

Per Diem

This payment method pays providers and caregivers a fixed amount per day. There are a number of variations. Sometimes there is a fixed payment for a procedure and a per diem rate for recovery days in the hospital. These mechanisms vary across markets, and the hospitals negotiate these payments directly with private insurers. In the US, roughly one-third of hospital payments are from private payers, and one primary form of private pay reimbursement is per diem (1).

Charges or Discounted Charges

Most hospitals, at least in the US, have something called a charge master. A charge master is a list of all of the goods and services that could possibly be consumed in the delivery of care along with a price for each of those goods and services. It is essentially a hospital price list. The items on the price list can range from one hour of operating room time to a bandage to a daily rate for a patient room. Some insurers negotiate a discounted charges contract with hospitals. These discounts can be in excess of 50 percent (2).

Patient Pay

Lastly, there is patient pay. In some markets, healthcare is still largely funded by patients. Patients can purchase insurance or decide to simply fund the cost of care when the need arises. In many developing markets, patient pay represents the primary form of payment. In some developed markets like the US, a small percentage of patients are patient pay either because they choose to or cannot afford insurance.

The type of system that the medical technology is being used in can have significant implication for price sensitivity and value. For example, if a new interventional cardiology technology is being launched, the company needs to think through the value and pricing carefully. The technology could have different value and price sensitivity if it is being launched into a patient pay versus a global budget market.

Coding, Coverage, and Payment

Reimbursement has three key elements. It is important to have a basic understanding of the three elements since each can have an impact on medical technology pricing. The three elements are coding, coverage, and payment. Each will be discussed in detail.

Coding

The first element of reimbursement is coding. Coding can be very complex, and it is not unusual for professional coders to specialize in just one area of coding such as in-vitro diagnostics coding or endovascular coding.

Even within one area such as in-vitro diagnostics, laboratory coding can vary widely between clinical chemistry and molecular diagnostics. In basic terms, coding is simply a means by which payers, caregivers, and asset owners communicate about what service was provided (procedure code) and why it was provided (diagnosis code).

As a simplified example, a physician may send a patient to have a CT scan for a suspicious lung mass that was previously spotted on an x-ray. In this case, the procedure code is the CT scan of the lung. The diagnosis code is a mass on lung. In the US, the CT scanner owner would bill the payer for the scan, and the physician who reads the scan may also bill. Coding becomes important for pricing since it can dictate how payers think about and pay for services and the technologies used to perform those services.

Coverage

The next element is coverage. Coverage simply means the payer can limit the reimbursement of or access to services that are provided to patients. Particularly for new technologies, it is not unusual for payers to not cover or to limit coverage. This is usually done because there is a lack of clinical evidence supporting the use of the technology.

In some countries, such as the United Kingdom, coverage decisions can also include an economic evaluation. The UK agency National Institute for Health and Clinical Excellence reviews and makes recommendations on the use and coverage of medical technologies and procedures. Other countries have similar technology assessment groups. In the US, some private payers use technology assessments that include both clinical and economic evaluation.

As an example, consider carotid artery stenting. Carotid artery stenting is a procedure and technology that was introduced about a decade ago. This procedure involves placing a self-expanding stent into the patient's carotid artery. A self-expanding stent is a tiny metal scaffold that expands when inserted into the patient's artery. It is used to clear a blockage in the artery. Prior to the development of this procedure, the standard of care was carotid artery surgery. This is a surgical procedure where the carotid artery is opened, cleaned out, and sutured shut. The stenting procedure is a less invasive procedure using catheter-based technology.

Although carotid artery stenting was a less invasive procedure, the issue with the new carotid artery stenting procedure was that it required a physician who is highly trained in catheter skills. A mistake in placement of the stent could mean that emboli or plaque could dislodge and be transported to the brain via the carotid artery. This could have significant adverse patient impact, which could include stroke.

Given the potential safety issues for the new procedure and based on clinical evidence, the Centers for Medicare and Medicaid Services (CMS) chose to limit coverage of the technology to a certain high-risk patient population at approval. So, based on clinical, and sometimes economic, evidence, payers can limit coverage to a subset of the market. This has to be considered when thinking through the pricing strategy (3).

In the US, the basis of coverage decisions by CMS is whether the procedure or therapy is reasonable and necessary. In evaluating whether a procedure, therapy, or technology is reasonable and necessary, CMS will explicitly take clinical evidence into account. This could lead to decisions to cover only certain patient populations. While economics are not explicitly considered in coverage decisions, it would be naïve to assume that the budget impact of a new technology, therapy, or procedure is not evaluated. This is particularly true for high-priced medical technologies. This means that a medical technology company facing a coverage decision should have some understanding of the potential budget impact of its technology.

Payment

Payment is the third element of reimbursement. Payment is the amount paid by the payer to the caregiver and asset owner for services rendered. There are a variety of systems and processes around the globe for determining payment amounts. For example, in the US inpatient Medicare payment system, hospitals are reimbursed via a diagnosis-related group (DRG). In the US and other countries on the DRG system, the DRG payment amount is often the reference hospitals look to when thinking about the price of existing or new technologies used for inpatient care.

Reimbursement Implications for Pricing

There are some obvious and less obvious reimbursement implications for pricing. Medical technology companies provide the goods and services that help caregivers and asset owners deliver healthcare services to patients. So, from a customer perspective, reimbursement is the revenue, and the medical technology is an input cost for providing the service. From a pricing perspective, there are five key reimbursement implications:

1. *Payment levels determine price sensitivity for products:* For both new and existing technologies and services, the actual reimbursement payment amount will drive customer price sensitivity. For example, if the reimbursement payment amount for a hip implant procedure is reduced by 10 percent, the hospital is going to look towards finding ways to reduce costs to make up for the lost reimbursement. Given the high nature of fixed costs for overhead and labor in hospitals, the administration will obviously look to finding ways to reduce the costs of supplies.

2. *Payment amounts help determine new technology adoption:* The payment amount will help determine the rate of new technology adoption. Asset owners and caregivers will base the decision on which patients use a new technology partly on the payment amount. If a medical technology innovator is introducing a new technology into a DRG that will cause the hospital to begin to lose money on the procedure, the hospital will likely limit use of the technology. This degree of constraint will depend on many factors, including available substitutes, the degree of unmet clinical need, and the total budget impact.

3. *Coverage decisions limit or expand the market:* The example of the carotid artery stent procedure discussed previously is a case where coverage decisions can limit or expand the market. In this case, the coverage decision intentionally limited technology access to one small segment of the patient population. Innovators would need to think through the implications for

pricing. If the value of the technology was much greater for the limited patient subset covered, this should be considered in the pricing strategy.

4. *Initial pricing can impact longer-term payments:* In some reimbursement systems, the basis of the system is cost. This is the current US Medicare system. A technology innovator has to be careful to not underprice the technology in hopes of driving adoption or creating a favorable financial situation for the asset owner. In this system, costs are used to determine reimbursement rates. So, a lower cost could lead to lower reimbursement over time. In addition, in the US, at the time of this writing, there are mechanisms in place to reimburse highly expensive new medical technologies with significant patient benefit. Underpricing these technologies likely make the technology ineligible for the add-on reimbursement. On the other hand, over-pricing the technology will likely lead to limited use.

5. *Getting coding right can help with pricing:* As was discussed previously, codes describe what service was provided and why it was provided. With many outpatient services, payment rates are assigned to the procedure codes. For inpatient services and some outpatient procedures, the diagnosis and procedure codes are used to assign the patient to a DRG in the inpatient setting or an ambulatory payment category (APC) for outpatient care. If a company has a new technology, it has to think through whether a code exists to adequately describe the service the technology will be used for and whether the associated payment is adequate. If the answer to either question is no, the company will have to consider applying for a new code. If the code is not appropriate, the company could be stuck with poor payment, which will impact pricing and utilization.

Assessing Reimbursement Situation

Better understanding the reimbursement implications for pricing starts with a basic assessment of the reimbursement situation. In general, the medical technology company needs to:

- *Understand site of service:* This simply means understanding where the technology will be used. Will it be used primarily in the hospital? Or is it a physician's office-based product?
- *Identify target markets:* This means identifying the target countries and markets where the product or solution will likely be launched.
- *Identify patient population:* The target patient population will drive value as well as other activities. Therefore, it is important to understand which patient population is the target for the product or solution.
- *Determine payer mix:* What is the payer mix for the type of technology? Is it private pay or government funded?
- *Evaluate reimbursement mechanics:* Is there currently coverage for the procedure, therapy, or diagnostic that the technology is used in? Are there any coding issues?
- *Assess payment levels:* Are the payment levels adequate to cover the value and price of the medical technology for the provider? Are the caregivers adequately reimbursed for their services?
- *Understand evidence requirements:* If changes are needed in coverage or payment levels, clinical and often economic evidence will be required. The medical technology company should be determining the evidence required to unlock reimbursement.

Importance of Evidence

Payers and governments are skeptical buyers. This is due to the significant pressure they are under as a result of demographic trends, rising healthcare costs, and existing government debt levels. It is not surprising that these stakeholders are becoming more demanding of the proof of value for new therapies, procedures, and technologies. This has obvious implications for medical technology companies.

Increasingly, payers are looking for both clinical and economic evidence to prove the utility and value of medical technologies. These data are helpful in making decisions on not just whether to fund a new procedure or technology but also on which patient populations to target with a new procedure or technology.

For example, studies show that the Center for Medicare and Medicaid Services' (CMS) coverage decisions are correlated with strength of evidence. In cases where there is poor evidence, the majority of the decisions are either to not cover or not expand coverage of the technology (4). Medical technology companies with expensive technologies with a potentially large target population should expect that the evidence standards will be even higher.

Figure 8.1 illustrates the connection between evidence, reimbursement, and pricing. Evidence positively impacts three areas, as shown in the chart. Strong evidence helps to drive the perceived value and willingness to pay. Next, evidence helps to unlock reimbursement by expanding coverage and influencing payment levels. Finally, all things being equal, stronger evidence helps to drive higher utilization of the technology. Indirectly, by unlocking reimbursement, evidence helps to drive both willingness to pay at a provider level as well as utilization. At times, increased utilization will impact price sensitivity and negatively impact willingness to pay. Clinical and economic evidence is the foundation for ensuring the medical technology company can capture a fair portion of the value it creates.

Figure 8.1 – Importance of Evidence

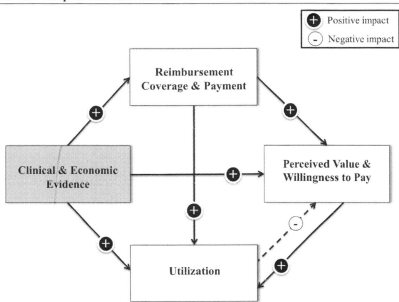

Case Study: ICDs in USA

The CMS coverage decision for implantable cardioverter defibrillators (ICDs) is an example of a coverage decision impacting the market. An implantable cardioverter defibrillator is a costly device for patients at high risk of sudden cardiac death. Heart disease may be complicated at any moment by a sudden, unexpected, and fatal abnormality of heart rhythm. A disorganized, chaotic rhythm termed "ventricular fibrillation" (VF) can occur. A person who develops VF has no effective circulation of blood to the body, which can lead to brain damage within minutes and death shortly thereafter (5).

ICDs are devices that constantly monitor the heart's rhythm, quickly detect development of VF, and deliver a lifesaving shock without need for outside intervention (6). These devices can cost upwards of $25,000. Manufacturers of these devices sought a broad coverage decision that would have substantially expanded the market for the technology.

157

Using data from a large study called MADIT-II, device manufacturers requested that CMS cover ICD implantation in a much broader population than was previously covered. The study showed that prophylactic use of ICDs resulted in a 31 percent reduction in mortality in the study population. Increasing the coverage to a broader patient population had the potential to add several billion dollars to annual health care costs. At the time, CMS decided to expand coverage but limit it to a narrower patient population than suggested by the study (7).

Case Study: Wound Healing Technology

Another example highlights the importance of clinical and economic evidence in funding and market development. The United Kingdom's National Institute for Health and Clinical Excellence (NICE) reviewed the MIST therapy system for the promotion of wound healing. The system consists of capital equipment and single use disposables and is aimed at promoting wound healing in hard-to-heal and acute wounds. It delivers low-energy, low-intensity ultrasound to the wound bed through a continuous saline mist. The mist is claimed to transmit the ultrasonic energy to the wound bed, to activate healing by the removal of slough, exudate and bacteria, and to stimulate tissue regeneration (8).

In reviewing the available evidence and the expert testimony, the committee conducting the review pointed out a number of issues with the clinical and economic evidence. These had to do with type of study, the methodology, and the ability to extrapolate findings across patient subgroups. The report stated that "the MIST Therapy system showed promise in the treatment of chronic wounds and its use was supported by expert opinion. The low quality of the evidence and consequent uncertainty about its relative effectiveness in healing wounds compared with standard care alone meant that the case for routine adoption in the NHS could not be supported at the time of writing." The committee recommended further research until it can support a recommendation for wider adoption (9).

The connection of evidence to reimbursement is critical. This is particularly true for expensive medical technologies as well as technologies that may be used more broadly. The more expensive a technology and the broader the usage, the more likely it is that the evidence standards will be very high. This is a critical point for pricing. If a medical company has a new technology that creates significant clinical and financial benefits, the company will likely want to capture a fair portion of that value through pricing. However, in order to actually achieve that price level, there has to be an investment in clinical and economic evidence.

Conclusion

Reimbursement is a critical element of pricing for medical technologies. Getting an adequate price for the technology or service you sell depends the coding, coverage, and payment. A lack of understanding or reimbursement planning can have the potential to significantly impact your prices and utilization. Likewise, poor initial pricing decisions impact reimbursement, which could drive utilization or longer-term pricing. There is a delicate balance between pricing, reimbursement, and evidence decisions. The goal here is not to "game" the reimbursement system or "maximize" reimbursement. Rather, the goal is to understand the system to be able to get paid a fair amount for the value that your technology brings to patients, payers, caregivers, and asset owners.

NOTES

1. Reinhart, U., (2006) The Pricing Of U.S. Hospital Services: Chaos Behind A Veil Of Secrecy. Health Affairs, 25, no.1 (2006):57-69

2. IBID

3. Decision Memo for Carotid Artery Stenting (CAG-00085R); www.cms.gov. accessed June 28, 2012

4. Neumann, P., Kamae, M., and Palmer, J., (2008) Medicare's National Coverage Decisions For Technologies, 1999–2007. Health Affairs, 27, no.6 (2008):1620-1631

5. Hlatky, M., Sanders, G., and Owens, D. (2005) Evidence-Based Medicine And Policy: The Case Of The Implantable Cardioverter Defibrillator. Health Aff January 2005 vol. 24 no. 1 42-51

6. IBID

7. IBID

8. The Mist Therapy System for the promotion of wound healing. July, 2011. www.nice.org.uk. accessed June 28, 2012

9. IBID

CHAPTER 9

UNDERSTANDING THE BUYING CENTER AND BUYING GROUPS

Understanding the supply chain strategy of your customers is a critical part of pricing. In healthcare, the supply chain strategy is simply the strategy the customer uses to procure goods and services that are used in the delivery of care. This strategy includes segmentation of supply items, sourcing processes, the approach to managing suppliers, and logistical decisions such as inventory management of supply items.

Supply sourcing strategies can also include decisions around the use of buying groups. Buying groups are groups of providers who aggregate purchasing for better terms. Whether the buying group is voluntary or controlled, they can have a varying degree of influence in product selection. There are many factors that drive the influence and impact that buying groups can have on a supplier.

Supply strategy and purchasing decisions are usually made by groups of people. These people are called a buying center. This group can include the user, a technical gatekeeper, economic buyers, and other influencers. The purchasing process and degree of influence of each of the members of the buying center can vary across type of supply item and type of institution and can vary over time within a given institution.

Understanding how your goods and services fit into the overall supply chain strategy is critical. It is also important to understand the nature of the buying center and how purchasing decisions are made. This chapter is meant to provide some perspective to the buying center and the purchasing decision process in provider organizations. It is also meant to disentangle buying groups and provide a framework for thinking strategically about buying groups.

Provider Purchasing and the Buying Center

Hospitals and provider organizations purchase thousands of supply items to deliver care. These range in price from a few cents per unit to millions of dollars for expensive capital equipment. The supply chain includes simple commodity items to highly differentiated physician preference items. In addition, studies have shown that more than 90 percent of supply items are slow moving, meaning ten or fewer of a particular item are used per day (1). The provider supply chain is a complicated area to manage.

From a holistic standpoint, the provider supply chain organization needs to consider a number of factors in the sourcing strategy.

- *Physician or user preference*: The role that physician or user preference plays in the purchasing decision.
- *Criticality of item*: The relative impact the supply item has on patient care and what would happen if it was not available.
- *Sources of supply*: This includes the number of suppliers or available substitutes.
- *Switching costs*: The cost to switch from one supplier to another, which includes the search and evaluation costs.
- *Budget impact*: The overall department or provider budget impact of spending on the supply item.

From a strategic standpoint, one of the ways to think about the provider supply chain and purchasing is to view this from a strategic sourcing perspective. Providers have thousands of supply items to purchase and manage. They also have hundreds or thousands of physicians and other caregivers who use the supply items. Keeping physicians and others aligned and satisfied is a key challenge. Therefore, simplifying the purchasing task while delivering savings, aligning clinicians, and delivering high-quality care is the goal.

Figure 9.1 provides a framework for thinking about purchasing from the provider perspective. This is adapted from general supply chain and strategic sourcing (2). On the vertical axis is total spending. On the horizontal axis is the supply characteristics. The supply characteristics are made up of the degree of physician or user preference, the availability of supply, switching costs, and the criticality of the item. There are four quadrants, each with a series of potential sourcing strategies.

Figure 9.1 is meant to provide a framework for thinking about pricing strategy within the context of the providers' supply chain strategy. The supply items that fall into the upper left corner are commodities. These are relatively high-budget spending areas where there is little clinician preference. Items in the upper right corner are strategic items. These are also high-budget spending items, but they have a high degree of physician or user preference. The lower right corner has items with relatively low budget but high preference. Finally, the lower left corner has low budget and low preference items.

Figure 9.1 – Supplier Segmentation & Sourcing/Cost Reduction Strategies

	Commodity	**Strategic**
	•Consolidate spend	•Align incentives
	•Use purchasing alliances	•Invest in relationship
	•Cost benchmarking	•Appropriate utilization
	•Supplier managed inventory	•Long-term agreements
		•Involvement in innovation
		•Leverage competencies
	Standard	**Key**
	•Consolidate spend	•Long-term agreements
	•Standardize purchasing	•Appropriate utilization
	•Use purchasing alliances	•Optimize supply chain
	•Minimize transaction costs	costs

Customer Characteristics — Spend — High / Low

Low ----------------	**Physician preference**	---------------- High
Many --------------	**Sources of supply**	---------------- Few
Low ----------------	**Switching costs**	------------------ High
Low ----------------	**Critical to care**	---------------- High

Supply Characteristics

The customer's sourcing strategy is likely to be different depending on the quadrant that your goods or services fall into. Likewise, the buying center, or group of people involved in making the purchasing decision, is likely to be different. For example, items that are considered commodities are more likely to have procurement or materials management play a more significant role in the decision process than items that are considered strategic. This should influence your pricing, offering, and value communication strategy.

From an overall supply chain and strategic sourcing perspective, the provider will likely take a different approach to sourcing the items that fall into each quadrant. For items that are in the commodity quadrant, the provider will look to consolidate spend, standardize, reduce inventory, and lower handling costs. Since supply items in this quadrant are relatively high-budget spending items, they naturally should receive a high degree of attention. The provider may also look to group purchasing organization (GPO) contracts as a means to standardize and reduce costs.

In recent years, providers and payers have become more sophisticated in attacking the costs and utilization of medical technologies. This is particularly true for high-cost, high-physician-preference items. In the US, for example, demonstration projects by CMS have shown that aligning incentives between physicians and hospitals reduces both prices and utilization of expensive physician preference items (3).

There are a number of sourcing tools and approaches providers can use to reduce costs, ensure appropriate utilization, and manage suppliers. Understanding these from a pricing and offering strategy perspective is important. These will be the tactics that your sales organization encounters in the buying process. The tools and approaches are as follows:

- *Consolidate spending:* Reduce the number of suppliers and consolidate spending to negotiate better pricing and terms.
- *Use purchasing alliances*: Use group purchasing organization (GPO) contracts to access more favorable pricing and terms.
- *Cost benchmarking:* Conduct frequent benchmarking of costs to identify savings opportunities.
- *Supplier-managed inventory*: Require suppliers to hold and manage inventory to reduce inventory carrying costs and costs associated with managing inventory.
- *Minimize transaction costs*: Use electronic ordering, inventory replenishment, and other tools to reduce transaction costs.
- *Appropriate utilization*: Align physicians and users on patient selection criteria and usage guidelines to manage expensive technologies.
- *Align incentives*: Use various mechanisms to align the financial interests of physicians with the provider.
- *Long-term agreements*: Negotiate long-term agreements to gain price concessions and to ensure supply.
- *Involvement in innovation*: Gain access to suppliers' innovation pipeline including access to clinical trials.
- *Invest in relationship*: Develop deep relationships with suppliers to leverage competencies and access resources.

- *Leverage competencies*: Seek to gain access to suppliers' competencies that can help the provider compete more effectively.
- *Optimize supply chain costs*: Ensure supply chain is managed to take costs out and to optimize cost position.

One of the ways providers choose to implement many of the tools mentioned above is through a value analysis committee. A value analysis committee is a cross-functional team made up of clinicians, materials management, department representatives, and finance (4). This committee is the buying center for many purchases. The goal of this committee is to help the provider:

- Make informed decisions about new technologies based on available clinical and economic evidence.
- Develop a formula or guidelines for the use of technologies in procedures in order to drive appropriate utilization.
- Identify cost-saving opportunities in the selection and use of medical technologies and supplies.
- Standardize supply items to reduce acquisition, handling, and storage costs of medical technologies and supplies.

The use, scope, and structure of these committees vary from provider to provider. The focus and names of these committees also vary across institutions. Some committees cover a wide array of clinical services and departments. Other committees cover just one area or department, such as surgery. In addition, there is still much debate about the right use and scope of these committees in the hospital marketplace (5). In the US, there is a professional society called the Association of Healthcare Value Analysis Professionals, which is dedicated to sharing insights and best practices in value analysis (6). The use and sophistication of these committees will grow as cost and reimbursement pressures continue.

From a provider perspective, the use of these committees makes a lot of sense. As mentioned previously, providers purchase thousands of supply items. These items vary widely in costs, usage patterns, clinician preference, and clinical impact. There are also new medical technologies launched all the time. Without a process and mechanism to manage product selection and purchasing, it is easy to imagine hospital supply costs getting out of control. For the medical technology company, the trick is understanding how the provider views your supply items as well as how the buying center and process works.

Drivers of Provider Buying Behavior

From a purchasing or material management perspective, there are five key organizational drivers of buying behaviors. These factors impact how the organization procures goods and services and their focus on price versus value in the purchasing equation. These five organizational buying behaviors are:

1. *Financial situation*: The financial situation of the provider organization will drive its buying behavior. Providers in relatively difficult financial situations will tend to be more price focused and less value based in their decision making. This could also impact the use and adoption of high-priced or new technologies.

2. *Procurement or material management maturity*: The maturity of the professional buying organization in the provider will drive the behavior. More mature and sophisticated organizations have a broader view of value and are willing to consider value in the buying decision. This does not mean that they will not test and push you in negotiations. It simply means that relative to a less sophisticated buyer organization, they will be more value oriented.

3. *Organizational buying rules*: Some organizations have specific rules and requirements for how they procure goods and services. This is particularly true for government-related organizations. Other organizations have implemented formal policies for the introduction of new technologies such as the use of value analysis committees.

4. *The type of supply or service you sell:* As was discussed above, many organizations segment supplies or suppliers into segments or categories. They have different sourcing strategies for the various categories.

5. *The organization's goals/strategies:* The goals and strategies of the organization as a whole often dictate how they treat suppliers and buy goods and services. Providers operating in highly competitive markets may be more interested in new technologies and creating new profitable service lines. Other providers may be more interested in participating in clinical studies.

Implications for Pricing and Offering Strategy

Understanding the customers' supply chain strategy, buying process, buying center, and buying behavior is critical for the pricing and offering strategy. For example, if your supply item is viewed as a commodity in the supplier segmentation model, you will need to think through the tactics and behaviors of the buyers. In this segment, buyers will look to consolidate vendors and reduce costs. You will need to be prepared to unbundle your offering and strip out as much cost as possible. Since customers will also be trying to consolidate vendors, your pricing strategy and pricing structure should reward customers who standardize and move market share and volume to you.

It is also important to understand that the market is not static. Since all technology follows a product life cycle, going from introduction eventually to decline, it is not unusual for the customers' sourcing strategy to change over time for a given medical technology. This often happens. When it does, it can catch the innovative company by surprise.

A medical technology company that launches a new type of technology may end up in the key or strategic quadrant in the beginning of the product life cycle. The technology is often a high physician- or user-preference item. It also has few direct competitors at that point. However, as time passes and the technology matures, there are more competitors. Customers become more familiar with the technology and require less support and training. Buyers then become more willing to take risks. It is at this stage that the buyer's view of the item switches from it being a strategic or key supply item to a commodity or standard item.

For the sales and marketing team, this change from a strategic or key item to a commodity or standard item usually means that the economic buyers play a much more influential role in purchasing. For organizations who are used to selling primarily to physicians and not dealing with economic buyers, this can be a shocking experience. Smart organizations prepare in advance by understanding the evolving market and how the customers' buying behavior will change. Armed with these insights, they work on developing an offering strategy, refining pricing, and preparing the organization to deal with the economic buyers.

Overview of Buying Groups

Purchasing alliances or buying groups are a key element of many providers' sourcing strategies. For purposes of this book, two broad types of buying groups will be defined. First, there are voluntary purchasing alliances. These are groups of end users (e.g., hospitals or laboratories) that can access contract terms and conditions that are negotiated by a purchasing alliance, usually a separate legal entity. Voluntary purchasing alliances operate much like retail stores Costco or BJ's. Members pay to join to gain access to special pricing and terms—at least that is the idea.

In the US, group purchasing organizations (GPO) represent a form of a voluntary purchasing alliance. GPO members gain access to the pricing and terms that are negotiated by the GPO. However, the members are generally not required to buy from the contract. Members of GPOs pay fees to the buying group. These members can also be owners or shareholders in the legal entity that does the contract negotiations on behalf of the buying group.

In addition to collecting fees from members, GPOs also collect fees from med tech companies for being on contract. These fees usually are around 1 to 3 percent of contracted sales. In 1986, US Congress created this safe harbor to allow GPOs to collect fees from manufacturers (7). GPOs' collection of fees from med tech companies and business practices have faced much scrutiny over the past decade or so. GPOs have faced US congressional investigations numerous times. This led the GPO industry to issue a voluntary code of conduct in 2002 (8). Therefore, it is important that med tech companies understand these purchasing alliances and how they operate to make well-informed strategic pricing decisions.

These type of entities were originally created as a mechanism to aggregate the purchasing power of many hospitals to negotiate better pricing. In fact, in 2011 the annual purchasing volume of the top five GPOs in the US range from seven to forty-five billion dollars (9). The substantial annual spending should give these entities significant leverage in negotiating better pricing and terms. However, some argue that because GPOs collect fees from both members and med tech companies, they do not act in the best interest of hospital members and miss savings opportunities (10).

The other type of buying group is a controlled purchasing alliance. In this case, there is a corporate entity that owns and controls the affiliates in the purchasing alliance. The affiliates can be subsidiaries of the corporate entity. Often, these are public corporations. In this case, the corporate entity makes supply decisions on behalf of the alliance, and it drives some level of compliance to the agreements. As with purchasing in any corporate environment with subsidiaries, the amount of control and standardization of purchasing can vary.

There are a number of proprietary owned hospital chains in the US that would meet the description of a controlled purchasing alliance. An example would be the public hospital corporation HCA. HCA owns roughly 167 hospitals (11). In the US, Europe, Asia, and Latin American, there are a number of commercial clinical laboratories that would meet this definition. These can be public corporations and non-public businesses. Examples would be Quest Diagnostics in the US, Labco in Europe, and Sonic Healthcare in Australia.

Integrated delivery networks (IDNs) in the US could also be considered controlled purchasing alliances. IDNs are groups of hospitals and other facilities such as surgical centers that are owned or controlled by a corporate entity. These entities classically provide care in a specific geographic area. IDNs can range in size from a few hospitals to over forty hospitals (12). Again, as with any corporate and subsidiary purchasing, there is a wide range of abilities to control and standardize purchasing across these entities.

Given the ability of these entities to aggregate purchasing power across hundreds or thousands of hospitals or labs, they often present a formidable challenge for med tech companies. The fear of losing big deals can often lead to irrational thinking and decisions on pricing. This doesn't have to be the case. Med tech companies need to understand the pros and cons of working with these entities and take a strategic perspective.

Approaching Buying Groups Strategically

From a strategic standpoint, negotiating deals with these purchasing alliances often comes with many pros and cons. There is not one right answer when making contracting and pricing decisions with purchasing alliances. The decision will depend on many factors, and it is up to the supplier to take a strategic perspective. This includes conducting the right analysis to understand the financial consequences of different contracting options.

Potentials Cons

- Given the aggregated purchase volume of its members, purchasing alliances should theoretically be able to negotiate better pricing than the individual members can by themselves on average. While this is listed as a con, there are some studies that show, and many argue, that voluntary purchasing alliance members can get better pricing on their own rather than through a voluntary purchasing alliance (13).

- Purchasing alliances often require an administration fee payment of 3 percent or more of contracted sales. This means that the med tech company has essentially added a 3 percent discount to pay for the administration fee.

- The purchasing alliance can often impose other terms of agreement that may be onerous or not ideal to the med tech company.

- For high physician preference items or new, novel technologies, many of the purchasing alliances do not have as much influence on purchase decisions.

Potential Pros

- Developing a broad agreement with the buying group often forces the med tech company to develop some basic pricing rules and to put some basic price discipline in place. Med tech companies fear that if they give special pricing to one member of the purchasing alliance, then they may be forced to give the same pricing and terms to other members. This often makes the special deal for one account look unattractive. Thus, it forces some price discipline.

- The purchasing alliance can provide efficiencies in contracting. Rather than negotiate pricing and terms with thousands of hospitals separately, the negotiated purchasing alliance pricing and terms can be used for all alliance members. This presumably reduces the cost of contracting and sales efforts to negotiate individual deals.

- Some of the purchasing alliances can also drive compliance to the terms of the agreement, which includes market share or volume commitments. This is a benefit of some alliances.

- Larger purchasing alliances provide a wide reach to many hospitals or other types of facilities that the med tech company may not want to call on. Therefore, the purchasing alliance can provide market access and in some ways could be considered an additional sales channel. It is not uncommon for some members of buying groups to simply follow the purchasing contracts of the alliance for many supply items. This is particularly true for smaller members.

So, taking a balanced perspective, there are many pros and cons for med tech companies to working with buying groups. For many of the controlled purchasing alliances, it is hard to not work with them. These are large entities with the power to move market share. Therefore, it is important to win business at terms that make sense financially. In the case of voluntary purchasing alliances like GPOs, the need to have a contract position with them will depend on the specific circumstances of your business.

Questions to Ask

In order to conduct an analysis of the merits of a contract position with a purchasing alliances, the following questions are offered to help think through the situation:

- How will being on contract or not being on contract impact patient access to your technology?
- What is the primary purpose of getting on contract with the purchasing alliance?
- Are the products you are selling more proprietary, high physician preference items?
- Can the purchasing alliance give access to hospitals or members who would be difficult to reach with your existing sales deployment and efforts?
- Will the purchasing alliance help to reduce your costs to contract and the cost of selling to the alliance members?
- Does the administration fee make sense in light of the benefits you will receive in exchange (e.g., lower costs or more volume or both)?
- Will being on contract provide some kind of strategic advantage relative to competition?
- If you choose not to contract with a purchasing alliance now, will that hurt your ability to do future deals with them?

Key Criteria to Assess and Segment Buying Groups

Beyond the general questions above, there are four key criteria to consider when assessing a buying group and making a decision on whether to enter into a contract. These are:

1. *Size:* How many members are part of the alliance? What percentage of members actually buy off of the purchasing alliance contracts? What is the annual contracted spending for the members?
2. *Control:* Does the purchasing alliance have mechanisms to control and drive compliance to the terms of the agreement? What are the mechanisms?
3. *Member mix:* What is the mix of members in terms of size, service offerings, location, and general buying behavior? Is this an attractive member mix based on your product offering? How does this impact your cost to serve?
4. *Group buying behavior:* How does the purchasing group normally act towards and treat suppliers? What is the typical buying process? What is the typical length of agreements?

Smart med tech companies have an ongoing process to assess the buying groups and prioritize and segment them. It is much more effective to think strategically about buying groups and how you want to approach them in advance. Waiting until the heat of the bid or tender can cloud decision making.

Figure 9.2 provides a framework to think about these groups. On the vertical axis is size in purchasing volume. This is the total potential business for the supply items that you are selling. On the horizontal axis is relative attractiveness. Attractiveness is driven by the factors two through four identified above.

In situations in the upper right corner, where it is a highly attractive buying group and is large in size, the supplier will want to focus on these and try to win at business terms that make sense. These are likely to be large customers who have the ability to move market share. These are difficult customers to ignore. Since they are large and attractive customers to you, they are often large and attractive to other suppliers. This means the business could be hotly contested. The supplier will need to be careful not to win at all costs.

The other quadrant that is relatively clear is the lower left corner. This is where it is a small buying group that is relatively unattractive. In this case, the right strategy might be to ignore them. It may not be worth the sales time and administrative effort to manage groups in this segment.

The other two quadrants are less clear. In these cases, the supplier will want to be selective. The decision to enter into contracts will be largely dependent on the specific circumstance. A smaller buying group that is attractive may be worth pursuing. Likewise, a large buying group that lacks control may not be worth having a contract with. The question in these cases becomes at what pricing and terms. At the right pricing and terms, customers in these quadrants could be worth having a contract with.

Figure 9.2 – Buying Group Segmentation

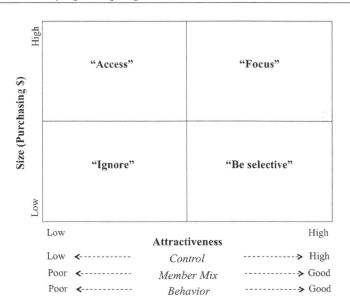

There is no right answer to the contracting strategy with buying groups. It really depends on the specific situation the med tech company is facing. For some companies and circumstances, having a contract with a voluntary purchasing alliance provides many benefits. In other situations, it provides few benefits. Medtronic made news in 2011 when it decided to cancel two billion dollars' worth of cardiovascular and spine contracts with Novation LLC, a group purchasing organization. It cited saving $60 million in administration fees (14). Medtronic decided to contract directly with the GPO members.

Conclusion

Developing and managing the pricing and offering strategy requires a clear understanding of the customers' sourcing strategy, buying center, and buying behavior. The customers' view of your supply items often dictates the sourcing strategy that they will implement. The customers' sourcing strategy often includes the use of purchasing alliances or buying groups. So, understanding the role, influence, and impact of the purchasing alliance in product selection is critical.

Providers are faced with the complex task of delivering a wide range of high-quality services while tightly managing costs. The medical technology company needs to determine how to help providers achieve these goals while still earning a reasonable profit and funding future innovations. Without a proactive approach to managing the offering and pricing strategy, this is a difficult challenge to meet.

NOTES

1. Cheng, S., and Whittemore, G., (2008) An Engineering Approach to Improving Hospital Supply Chains. Masters Thesis. www.dspace.mit.edu accessed June 28, 2012.

2. Adapted from: Bueler, D., (2006) Supplier Segmentation – The Tool for Differentiation and Results. 91st Annual International Supply Management Conference. May 2006

3. Ketcham, J. and Furukawa, M. (2008) Hospital-Physician Gainsharing In Cardiology Health Aff. May 2008 vol. 27 no. 3 803-812

4. Barlow, R., (2010) Redefining value analysis practices for a healthcare reform-minded industry. Healthcare Purchasing News October, 2009. accessed June 29, 2012

5. IBID

6. The Association Of Value Analysis Professionals (AHVAP). Ahvap.org

7. See details at http://www.medicaldevices.org/issues/GPO-Reform. Accessed June 28, 2012

8. Walsh, M. (2009) Senators Investigate Hospital Purchasing. NY Times Published August 13, 2009. accessed June 28, 2012

9. See Healthcare Purchasing News, GPO facts and figures. http://www.hpnonline.com/resources/GPOs.html accessed June 28, 2012

10. MDMA Statement on Senator Grassley and GAO Reports Showing No Evidence of Cost Savings by GPOs. September 27, 2010. www.medicaldevices.org . accessed June 28, 2012

11. Healthcare Purchasing News, GPO facts and figures. http://www.hpnonline.com/resources/GPOs.html, accessed June 28, 2012

12. IBID

13. Blake, M. (2010) Dirty Medicine. Washington Monthly. July-August 2010. Accessed June 28, 2012.

14. Baucus Investigates Medtronic to Ensure Patients, Hospitals Don't Bear Increased Costs. May 2, 2011. www.senate.finance.gov. accessed June 28, 2012

CHAPTER 10

INNOVATION STRATEGY AND PRICING

The medical technology industry is a critical player in improving human healthcare. From a societal perspective, there are a number of diseases and conditions that are still poorly understood, lack adequate diagnostics, and do not have good treatments. Consider the current state of cancer diagnosis and treatment. Despite all of the advancements in cancer treatment, there are still many types of cancer for which we not only lack good treatments, but for which we also lack a clear understanding of the underlying disease mechanism (1). There are many areas of healthcare where medical technology innovators can play a role in improving patient quality of life, reducing costs of care, and extending people's lives.

This chapter is meant to provide some perspective for how to think about value and pricing as it relates to medical technology innovation. It first starts with defining innovations from a pricing and value perspective. Next, there is a section that addresses how to consider value and price in the innovation strategy decisions. Finally, a process for integrating value and pricing into the new product development process will be reviewed. Getting innovation right and capturing a fair portion of value is critical to both the medical technology company as well as patients and society.

Part of a successful innovation strategy is making smart decisions about which innovations to fund and how to capture value. This is becoming more important as the cost of developing and bringing new technologies to market increases. This is due, in part, to higher regulatory hurdles and increasing development costs. The need to make smarter investments and value capture decisions is also growing as economic buyers play an increasingly important role in product selection and funding decisions both at a provider and payer level.

Therefore, medical technology innovators need to pay close attention to value in making choices about which innovations to fund and develop. They also need to carefully consider value and pricing throughout the product development process. The days of launching products or technologies with a few new features and hoping for a higher price and market share are largely over. Innovators need to understand the value of those features and be able to convince payers and providers to pay more based on the outcomes delivered.

The root cause of many new product commercial failures and the pricing issues a firm faces can often be traced back to poor innovation decisions or a lack of the right value-defining processes in product development. For example, it is not unusual for technology companies to over-engineer products beyond what the customer is willing to pay for. In the pursuit of adding product features, the company can end up with a product that is over-engineered with a high manufacturing cost. The company then often sets a cost-based price at a point that is beyond what mainstream customers are willing to pay. The feedback from the market comes in the form of pricing pressure. Discounting ensues, and the company's profitability suffers. This phenomena will increase in the future as economic evaluation of medical technologies becomes even more important.

Types of Innovation and Pricing Implications

The type of new product or solution should drive how the med tech innovator thinks about pricing and value for the innovation. There are many ways that businesses think about and characterize innovations. Many businesses use terms such as incremental, substantial, or disruptive to characterize innovations. Often, the terms are used differently even within the same business.

For the sake of clarity, from a pricing and value standpoint, four broad types of innovations will be defined. The reason for separating the innovations into four separate groups is because the approach to pricing and value can differ for each group. Given the many complexities of the healthcare system, the type of the innovation plays a significant role in its value potential and the way that innovators should think about pricing.

For example, a technology that is a substitute in an existing procedure usually has an established payment mechanism, a payment amount, and existing provider economics. Whereas a technology that is creating an entirely new procedure or service will require a payment mechanism, funding, and an understanding of the provider and physician economics. Thinking about pricing and value is different depending on the type or nature of the innovation.

The type of innovation also can have a profound impact on the commercial activities of the firm. These activities include areas such as investments in clinical data, user training requirements, reimbursement, publication strategies, pricing, and other market-building activities. The four categories of innovation are:

1. *Substitute product:* This is a new product that is a substitute for an existing product used in an established procedure or diagnostic service. This could be a new device that replaces an existing device in laparoscopic hernia surgery, as an example. In the case of a substitute, there is already an existing procedure or service with reimbursement, and a set of provider and physician economics. Usually, the evidence requirements for a new substitute product can be much lower. In this situation, the innovator needs to understand the clinical and economic value created by the new technology relative to the technology it replaces. The value analysis should consider procedure costs, in-hospital costs, and appropriate follow-up costs. The value analysis should also consider any positive or negative impacts to clinical outcomes.

2. *Enabling technology or service:* In this case, there is an existing procedure or service. The new product or service is added to

the procedure or service to enable the core technology. The core technology is the critical value-creating technology that is used in the procedure or service. It would be helpful to consider a couple of examples of enabling technologies. In a cardiac ablation procedure, catheters—long, flexible tubes inserted through a vein in the groin and threaded to the heart—are used to correct structural problems in the heart that cause an arrhythmia (2). A special machine sends energy to the heart through one of the catheters. The energy destroys small areas of heart tissue where abnormal heartbeats may cause an arrhythmia to start (3). The core technology is the machine and catheters. Enabling technologies could be the software used to map the treatment area. Enabling technologies and services work by improving the cost, time, or quality of the core technology. Automation in the clinical laboratory setting could be considered enabling technology. In this case, the core technology is the reagents and instruments used to develop a test result. Automation serves to improve the cost, time, and quality of the core technology. Often, as the core technology matures and becomes good enough, the basis of competition becomes the financial impact or efficiency of performing the procedure or service. This is when the enabling technologies become critical.

3. *Additive product:* In this case, there is an existing procedure or service. The new product is added to the procedure or service to improve clinical outcomes or to positively impact downstream costs. It is not substituting for an existing supply item and is not enabling the core technology to do its job better, faster, or cheaper. Many diagnostic services fall into this category. An example would be a CT scan used to rule out ischemic stroke for a patient who just entered the emergency room and is later admitted to the hospital. In this case, there are reimbursement and payment rates in place for treatment of a stroke patient. The scan is used in addition to other existing diagnostics to improve the diagnosis. The challenge for the innovator is to

prove that the new product has enough clinical and economic value to warrant the additional costs.

4. *New product/new procedure:* In this case, the new product is used to enable a new procedure or type of diagnostic service. Minimally invasive gall bladder surgery is an example. Prior to the advent of minimally invasive instruments, gall bladder removal was performed with an open surgical procedure. The introduction of endoscopes, trocars, and other devices helped to enable the new minimally invasive procedure. Usually, but not always, reimbursement is a significant issue, and the innovator will need to gather both clinical and economic data to unlock reimbursement.

Role of Value and Pricing in Innovation Strategy

Usually, medical technology innovators develop new products and solutions to address some unmet need or to help clinicians perform some job that needs to be done. The hope is that solving the unmet need or performing the job better than competitors will lead to an advantage and higher sales and profits. Given the complexities of value interpretation, the different stakeholders involved, and the peculiarities of the payment systems, chasing after unmet needs without a lens to think about value and pricing can result in poor investment decisions.

In order to help simplify the innovation decisions from a value perspective, it is helpful to consider two key dimensions or vectors of differentiation for assessing value. In his book on innovation, McGrath discusses vectors of innovation. Innovation can occur as sustained improvement in differentiation along a distinct path or vector (4). Depending on the marketplace, these vectors of differentiation could include areas such as ease of use, customer benefits, total cost of ownership, product performance, or convenience.

Amazon is great example of innovation along the dimension of convenience. Amazon provides numerous differentiated convenience benefits as compared to a regular bookstore. These benefits include things like the ability to purchase books without traveling to the bookstore, free advice on which books to buy, instant access to opinions and research, history of your purchases, and storage of e-books that are purchased.

In healthcare, from a value and pricing perspective, there are two primary vectors of differentiation to innovate along. These are clinical outcomes/performance and financial impact/efficiency. Clinical outcomes represent improvements in clinical endpoints such as safety, effectiveness, and quality of life. It is also meant to capture improvements in clinical performance of technologies that help lead to improvements in clinical endpoints. An example would be a new type of CT scanner that provides even greater performance in terms of ability to diagnose patient disease.

Next, financial impact and efficiency is the other dimension to consider. This is the financial impact of using the technology or service for whoever is paying for it. Financial impact is meant to capture the economic value as was discussed in chapter three from the provider or payer perspective. The financial impact is also meant to take into account the overall economics of the provider, which includes reimbursement.

Putting these two dimensions or vectors together results in Figure 10.1. Using Figure 10.1 as a framework, let us consider an innovation decision a company may be contemplating. In this simplified example, there are two competitors, A and B. Competitor A has a solution that provides better clinical outcomes/performance, but it is not as attractive from a financial perspective. Assume competitor A is considering multiple potential investment decisions. It could improve the clinical performance of the existing technology and move to position number 1. Alternatively, it could develop a lower cost-flanking product to move to position number 2. From an innovation standpoint, both of these choices would be developing a substitute technology for an existing product. Finally, the company could invest in enabling technologies that improve the cost and efficiency of the core technology to move to position number 3.

Figure 10.1 – Innovation & Value

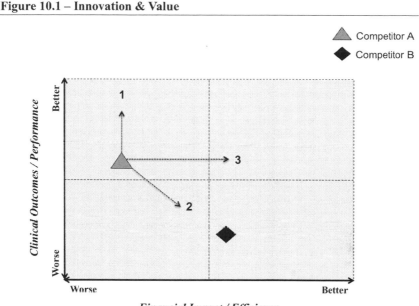

Financial Impact / Efficiency

Medical technology companies face these type of choices all the time. In the imaging segment, manufacturers of CT scanners face the decision of whether to develop the next-generation technology that improves the image quality and speed or to develop lower-priced technologies that are good enough for certain markets and segments. Obviously, each of the potential decisions has a range of investments, different regulatory hurdles, and other strategic considerations.

However, each potential choice should first be evaluated from a customer value perspective. Innovation choice number one would imply that further clinical improvements would result in measurable benefits and that there is a large unmet clinical need. Companies that over-innovate in this direction fall into the innovators' dilemma that Christensen describes in his book (5). In a constant attempt to improve technology performance, they end up over-innovating and become vulnerable to lower cost, inferior, or "good enough" technologies.

Innovation choice number two assumes that competitor B is a potential threat and that at least some portion of the market believes that an inferior product is good enough. Developing a lower-cost-flanking product would provide the strategic flexibility to address a lower-cost competitor and also target different segments of customers with differing needs. It could be that the target markets are developing nations without the infrastructure to handle the higher-performance technology. Alternatively, it could be that the target market for competitor B is a specific patient subset that does not need the added performance that competitor A's existing technology currently provides.

From a pricing and economic value perspective, the choice of which vector to further innovate along, whether clinical outcomes/performance or financial/efficiency, requires answering some critical questions:

- What type of innovation is being considered—substitute, enabling, additive, or new product/new procedure?
- What is the value of making further improvements in clinical outcomes/performance for the disease or condition?
- Is there a large unmet clinical need for certain segments or markets?
- At what point are clinical outcomes/performance considered "good enough" for most of the market?
- How will the innovation impact the financials of the provider, payers, and physicians?
- At what stage of the technology life cycle is the market?
- What will be the basis of competition in the future in this market—further clinical improvements or improvements in financial impact/efficiency?

As markets mature and the core technology becomes good enough, the basis of competition often changes. Consider clinical laboratory testing. For many routine blood tests, manufacturers have improved the core technology—the instruments and reagents—to the point where the tests are good enough. In recent years, many manufacturers have moved to improving the efficiency and financial impact of performing these routine tests. This has been done through enabling technologies. In the case of routine blood testing, this has been done through automation equipment and informatics solutions. Robotic and track technology is used to take out routine, non-value-added tasks. Informatics solutions are used to improve the efficiency of capturing, storing, and transmitting test results. Together, these technologies help to move routine blood testing innovation along the vector of financial impact/efficiency. Therefore, the innovation strategy needs to carefully consider pricing and value when making choices about how to win in the future.

Integrating Pricing and Value into Product Development

Frequently, med tech innovators are faced with a number of decisions during the product's development that can impact the price of the new product. These decisions can have an impact on the price potential and the overall price levels of the product or solution, particularly for new innovative technologies. The decisions include:

- What will be the first intended use or indication they will seek for the new technology?
- What will be the initial target patient population?
- If they have a choice, what regulatory path will they follow to gain approval to market the new technology?
- What countries will the technology be launching in, and what will be the sequence of launch?
- What type of clinical and economic evidence will be developed beyond what is required to gain regulatory approval?

Often, in the quest to get to market quickly, med tech innovators choose the least burdensome regulatory path and will invest in evidence just to gain approval. While this may have advantages in speed to market from a pricing standpoint, it can cause issues. The decision to take the quickest path to market can often cause the following issues:

- *New product lacks evidence:* The company may end up with adequate evidence to gain regulatory approval but have a deficit of evidence in being able to convince customers, payers, and others of the value of the technology. For example, it is not unusual for payers to have a high standard in terms of the evidence they need to grant incremental reimbursement or change a reimbursement coverage decision. It is not unusual for medical technologies to gain regulatory approval to market a new product but have payers unwilling to pay for a technology due to lack of evidence.

- *Low value indication or use is chosen:* The quest to get to market quickly may mean that the company chooses to gain approval for a low value indication or use. The price potential of the new technology will reflect this lower value. When the company eventually gains approval for the higher value use, the price is already set, and it is often difficult to change.

- *Launch in low-price markets:* There is also the choice of where to launch first. It is not unusual for companies to try to launch in Europe first since it is often perceived as an easier place to get to market. However, the price levels for medical technologies in Europe tend to be generally lower. While this is not always the case, it is often true. As a result, a choice to launch in Europe first means the company sets price levels at the European level. This can have implications for price levels in other parts of the world. So, the choice of where to launch first and the sequence of launch can impact pricing.

There is no right approach or right answers to deal with the issues outlined above. The medical technology innovator will have to balance speed to market, the competitive situation, costs, and other factors when making a decision of where to launch, which indications to focus on, and what regulatory path to follow. However, the innovator should be aware of the pricing and value issues and make a well-thought-out decision.

New Product Pricing Process

Given the regulated nature of the industry, medical devices and diagnostics companies must have a formalized new product development process. While the processes are different across firms, at a high level, many companies have some kind of stage gate process like those first introduced by Dr. Robert Cooper. Cooper defines five stages: Preliminary Investigation, Detailed Business Case, Development, Testing and Validation, and Full Production and Market Launch (6).

Most companies with a good new product development (NPD) process have clearly defined the inputs, outputs, process steps, and criteria for each stage of product development. Numerous studies across many industries indicate the clear importance of integrating marketing and other functions into the NPD process. In fact, one study shows that better integration results in improved market success (7). Moreover, the same study indicates that for highly innovative products, integration early in the NPD is particularly important. These insights should not be surprising and the information should be fairly transferable to the medical devices and diagnostics industry.

Given the numerous stakeholders involved, the growing evidence requirements, and the increase in value-based purchasing at entities from hospital to payers, the ability to do value-based pricing is critical. Yet, in practice, many firms have not or have poorly defined the role of different functions in the NPD process as it relates to value and pricing. Regardless of how the company is organized, there should be clearly defined value pricing deliverables and key questions to ask at each stage of the NPD process. Table 10.1 offers a framework that provides the critical deliverables for and key questions to ask at each stage.

For example, early in the detailed business case development stage, someone in the organization needs to help estimate the potential customer economic value of certain features under consideration. This can then be compared with the estimated cost to develop and manufacture those features to help the organization make trade-off decisions prior to full development. Usually, the last thing the organization wants to do is develop a new technology with features that cost much more to manufacture than the value that these same features create for customers. Yet, without a robust process, this is a mistake that a company can easily make.

Likewise, the organization needs to be asking what evidence is required to substantiate value very early in the stage gate process. It is not enough that the company has an understanding of the value of the innovation. A great real life case is Johnson and Johnson's drug-eluting coronary artery stent. J&J was charging nearly triple the price of bare metal stents and backed up the price with clear clinical and economic data to defend the value of the technology. The wealth of evidence must have taken considerable pre-planning and surely didn't happen by accident.

Table 10.1: Integrating Value and Pricing into New Product Development

Stage	Preliminary Investigation	Detailed Business Case	Development	Testing & Validation	Market launch
Key value questions	◊What are customers' key value drivers? ◊Solving which unmet needs generate the greatest value? ◊Based on value and costs, which features should be priority for development?	◊What is the potential value of the technology? ◊Which indications might be a priority? ◊What is reimbursement situation for innovation? ◊What evidence will be needed to support value & reimbursement?	◊What activities will be required to unlock reimbursement? ◊What published data will be required to support value?	◊What is value based on new data? ◊What value selling tools are required to defend value?	◊What should be the pricing strategy? ◊How will value selling tools be deployed to defend value? ◊Is evidence clearly aligned to value?
Critical value deliverables	◊Customer value drivers analysis ◊Potential value of key points of difference	◊Preliminary value estimate ◊Price potential ◊Evidence plan ◊Preliminary reimbursement assessment	◊Updated value analysis ◊Reimbursement strategy ◊Publication strategy	◊Preliminary pricing strategy ◊Updated value analysis ◊Reimbursement plan	◊Final pricing strategy ◊Value selling tools ◊Evidence dossier ◊Field training plans

Pricing and New Product Adoption

One of the more misunderstood and trickier issues to deal with is new product pricing and its impact on the rate of adoption of the new technology. When a new product's sales are below expectation, the focus often turns to pricing as the key driver of the underperformance. The innovator will lower the price only to see little incremental sales volume. While there are times when pricing will limit adoption of a new technology, the role of pricing and other factors in product adoption is often misunderstood.

It is often helpful to think about medical technology adoption from a diffusion of innovation perspective. Innovation diffusion researchers have studied the adoption of innovations across a broad spectrum of industries and circumstances. Many of these studies focus on healthcare and medical technologies. In his book on the diffusion of innovation, Everett Rodgers outlined five key attributes of new technologies that impact adoption (8):

1. *Relative advantage:* The degree to which the innovation is perceived as being better. In the case of medical technologies, this would include clinical, economic, and psychological benefits. This is where reimbursement plays a critical role. A technology that is clinically superior but lacks adequate reimbursement or has coverage issues will encounter problems.
2. *Compatibility:* The degree to which the innovation is perceived as consistent with values, past experiences, and needs. For new medical technologies, this could also include compatibility with processes, treatment protocols, and physician society guidelines.
3. *Complexity:* The degree to which innovation is perceived as difficult to understand and use. In the case of medical technologies, this can include items like the training required and ease of use.
4. *Trialability:* The degree to which the innovation can be used or trialed on a limited basis.
5. *Observability:* The degree to which the results of an innovation are visible to others. In the case of medical technologies, this

would obviously include clinical and economic data illustrating the safety, effectiveness, and economic value of the technology.

Without an understanding of diffusion of innovation drivers, medical technology companies face the risk of pointing to pricing as the barrier of adoption. While it can certainly play a part in limiting demand, as you can tell from above, there are many other product characteristics that drive adoption of new technologies. Many of these factors have little or nothing to do with the price level.

Conclusion

The medical technology industry thrives on innovation. Innovation is critical to the future growth of the industry, and the industry plays a key role in helping to solve unmet medical needs. Yet, the industry faces a number of trends—such as the aging population, government budget crisis, and overall healthcare costs—that will impact innovation. These trends should have an impact on how innovators think about where they place their bets and what work is done to develop a value story and choose a pricing strategy. For successful companies, value and pricing will need to be critically integrated into the innovation process and thinking. The days of launching new products with marginal feature improvements and expecting a price premium are largely over.

NOTES

1. Christensen, C., Grossman, J., and Hwang, J. (2009) The Innovators Prescription. New York, NY: McGraw Hill.
2. What is Catheter Ablation? www.nhlbi.nih.gov/health/health-topics/topics/ablation/. accessed June 28, 2012
3. IBID
4. McGrath, M. (2001) Product Strategy for High Technology Companies. New York, NY: McGraw Hill.
5. Christensen, C., Grossman, J., and Hwang, J. (2009) The Innovators Prescription. New York, NY: McGraw Hill.
6. Cooper, R. (1999) Product Leadership. New York: Perseus Books
7. Song, M., and Swink, M. (2009) Marketing–Manufacturing Integration Across Stages of New Product Development: Effects on the Success of High- and Low-Innovativeness Products. IEEE Transactions on Engineering Management Vol. 56, NO. 1
8. Rodgers, E., (1995) Diffusion of Innovation. (4th ed.): The Free Press New York, NY.

CHAPTER 11

INTERNATIONAL MEDICAL TECHNOLOGY PRICING

Healthcare is different around the world. The structure of the markets, the role of government in payment and coverage decisions, and the economics of delivering care all vary across markets. These inherent differences also drive variation in willingness to pay. The result can often be widely divergent prices for medical technologies across markets.

Is this something to worry about? How should global firms approach managing prices in different markets? This chapter will explore the issues, provide an analytical framework, and discuss possible ways to mitigate and manage the impact of price variations across markets.

Drivers of Price Differences

What drives price differences across markets? There are a number of factors. Some are company related, such as how the firm decides to manage pricing. Other factors are the result of the external environment. Finally, a number of the factors are the result of the unique characteristics of each market. The net result is price differences across markets that have to be monitored, assessed, and often actively managed. Figure 11.1 provides a summary of the factors (1).

Figure 11.1 – Drivers of Price Variation

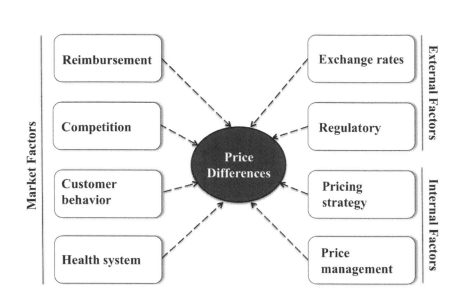

The first category of factors are market related. These include reimbursement, competition, customer behaviors, and the dynamics of the health system. The combination of these factors are often key drivers of price variation across markets. The market factors are difficult to control, but med tech companies can certainly mitigate the risk if they are clever.

The first market factor is reimbursement. Reimbursement systems and payment amounts vary by country. It is not unusual for different counties in the same region to reimburse the same product at reimbursement payment rates that are 100 to 500 percent different between markets. This means that the customer's economics and willingness to pay will vary widely across markets.

Next is competition. Competition dynamics and the level of competitive intensity is often different in each market. There are a variety of reasons for this. Often, it can be due to the goals, personalities, and histories of each competitor in the market. For example, in one industry, the German market tended to be fiercely competitive relative to other markets. One of the key drivers for competitive intensity in Germany was the fact that two of the competitors were headquartered or had significant presence in the country. Each wanted to be market leader in what they considered their home market.

Customer behavior and structure differs across markets. Customers in certain markets have higher expectations and needs as it relates to quality. Japan is an example of where customers' expectations for service and product quality usually exceed that of other markets. Also, the size and structure of healthcare customers often differ across markets. Some markets have a higher concentration of very large customers, whereas others have many smaller customers.

In addition, the healthcare system in each market varies. The country's willingness to pay for certain diseases and conditions can be different. This is driven by societal factors such as the prevalence of certain diseases, strength of physician societies, patient advocacy groups, and the cost to deliver care in that market. This means a technology that delivers a certain improvement in length of stay, for example, would create different savings in the United States compared with Brazil. Therefore, variances in the healthcare systems inherently create different value and willingness to pay across markets.

Another source of price variation is external factors. These include exchange rate changes and the regulatory environment. The biggest of the two is exchange rate changes. With a sudden currency devaluation, the prices of products in a given country can quickly decline relative to other markets. If these same products are sold in other parts of the world, this devaluation could create potential price reference and parallel trade issues.

Internal company processes and decisions also may be a root cause of price differences. These differences usually start with pricing strategy. The company could lack a clear pricing strategy, or the pricing strategy may not be coordinated across markets. Global firms often lack a coordinated approach to establishing pricing strategy for each market for a given product. In many companies, the choice of strategy is left up to the local country management. This means that two bordering countries could have very different pricing strategies. As a result, price levels for the same product could vary significantly. For example, France may choose penetration pricing for a particular product, while Germany may choose a skim-pricing strategy for the same product. The result may be widely differing price levels in the two countries.

Another potential driver of price variation across markets is poor price management. It is not uncommon for prices to vary by 200 to 300 percent from one market to the next simply as a result of the countries not having good pricing policies, rules, and price controls in place. This means that poor price management in one country has the potential of impacting many different countries.

Figure 11.2 shows how pricing strategy and pricing implementation impact each other as it relates to global pricing risk. When pricing strategy is coordinated but price implementation is poor, the company still has significant risk. This is represented in the lower left cell.

Likewise, if the company has implemented good price management processes but strategy is uncoordinated, the result can be trouble. There could be excellent process and price management in place, but the price strategy and levels are not coordinated. The global reference risk still exists. This is represented by the upper right cell. When strategy is not coordinated and price management is poor, there certainly presents a much higher level of risk.

Figure 11.2 – Price Strategy & Implementation Impact

		Pricing Strategy	
		Coordinated	*Uncoordinated*
Pricing Implementation / Management	*Excellent*	**Success** • Risk of price arbitrage and price referencing minimized	**Trouble** • Prices well managed, but strategy not coordinated • Still represents potential risk due to price referencing or price arbitrage risk
	Poor	**Trouble** • Pricing strategy coordinated across markets, but poor price management • Still a price reference and price arbitrage risk	**Mess** • Strategy not coordinated and price management poor • Represents significant potential risk • Harder to fix since two separate issues need to be addressed

The prior two factors are the result of internal decisions a company makes on pricing strategy, price management processes, and the overall organization philosophy regarding pricing. These are relatively easy to manage and address compared to other drivers. The combination of the internal company factors and the external environment means that prices will naturally vary across markets if they are not managed. This variation can be significant. For example, prior to the introduction of drug-eluting stents, the price differences in bare metal coronary stents across markets varied from $200 to $1500 per stent—more than a 700 percent difference across markets (2).

Identifying and Evaluating Risk

Should medical technology firms worry about wide price variations across markets? There are a number of potential reasons to be concerned about price variations. Customers, payers, and gray traders can all take advantage of price differences, which could impact a firm's prices and profits. There are five key potential areas of risk, summarized in Table 11.1.

Table 11.1 – Sources of Risk

Source of risk	Type of Risk	Description
Global customers	Price referencing	Customers who operate in different countries around the world. This means the customer can easily benchmark prices in various markets.
Payers	Price referencing	Payers who can benchmark or reference reimbursement rates and prices in different markets. Since health technology assessments are often shared across markets, this is a source of real risk.
Free-trade regions	Price arbitrage	Regions with free-trade treaties that allow free movement of goods across markets.
Small user community	Price referencing	Small community of product users who have potential to discuss pricing at meetings.
Distributors	Price arbitrage	Distributors who purchase products in one market and sell the product in another to take advantage of price arbitrage.

One of the most dangerous areas of risk is customers who operate across borders. Naturally, these customers have access to prices in each of the markets where they operate. This is particularly true in some parts of the medical technology industry, such as in in-vitro diagnostics. In this marketplace, there are customers who own clinical laboratories in numerous countries in a given region such as Europe. There are also customers who operate laboratories across various continents. This means that the customers will have access to and be able to capitalize on variation in prices across markets.

Another source of potential price referencing risk is payers. It is not unusual for payers to conduct or sponsor health technology assessments. These assessments often include data about the price or cost of the medical technology. The global payer community often shares these assessments. So, in a sense, they are sharing pricing information across markets. This is particularly true of expensive new technologies. This is exactly what happened with one new technology.

Case Example: DES Price Referencing

During the commercialization of the first drug-eluting stent in the United States, the Center for Medicare and Medicaid Services (CMS), decided it was going to cover and reimburse the new technology at the time of FDA approval. However, CMS had no standard process to set reimbursement rates for new technologies prior to FDA approval. So, the head of CMS at the time, Tom Scully, looked at the prices for the new drug-eluting stent in the United Kingdom in order to set the reimbursement rate in the United States. CMS used international price referencing to set reimbursement in the United States (3).

Another risk is free-trade zones like the European Union. In this example, the free-trade law prohibits interfering with the free flow of goods across the union. This means that it is legal to buy products in one country and sell in another. The issue of goods flowing from one market to another is particularly troublesome in markets like pharmaceuticals where the products are of very high value and relatively easy to transport.

The user community of the technology also has the potential to generate price referencing across markets. Many physician societies, for example, have congresses that are attended by physicians from around the world. This means that there is the potential for exchange of not just scientific data, but also insights and information on commercial practices of companies across the world. Take, for example, the interventional neuroradiology specialty. This is a physician specialty with a relatively small user community. In the United States alone, it is estimated that the community is approximately a couple of hundred specialists (4).

Finally, distributors who operate in more than one country present the risk of acquiring product in one market and selling it in another to take advantage of price differentials across markets. Otherwise known as gray trade, this activity can significantly impact the profits of medical technology companies. Sometimes this is perfectly legal in markets where regulatory and free trade is not an issue.

In all of the cases mentioned previously, the root cause was wide differences in prices across markets for the same product. Sometimes this presents a reference price risk. This is where the user or customer uses the information to pressure the supplier for better prices. Other times, the price differences result in arbitrage and the physical flow of product from one market to the other. In either case, the result is lost profits for the seller.

Evaluating Risk

How do med tech firms evaluate the risk of global pricing? There are a number of questions to try to answer:

- Are there wide price differences across markets?
- Are there customers who operate across borders?
- Is there the potential for new cross-border customers?
- Are the products high value and easily transported?
- Could a third party earn a good profit by buying your product in one market and selling in another?
- Do payers exchange technology assessments in your markets?
- Do the technology users regularly attend congresses together across markets?
- Is there a high need for service and support to use the offering?

- Are there regulatory barriers preventing the flow of goods from one market to another?

The exercise of evaluating the risk of differences in global prices has to start with an analysis of the actual market prices. The analysis needs to assess not just the average price in the market but also the range of prices. Since the customer will not know your average prices but instead will see only an invoice or quoted price, the risk is the entire range of pricing in the market.

The analysis of global pricing can be a significant undertaking. This is particularly true when the company has thousands of product codes. However, there are a number of approaches to simplify the analytical exercise. First, the firm should do an 80/20 analysis and identify the approximately 20 percent of the product codes that generate 80 percent of the revenue. It is not uncommon for companies with thousands of product codes to find just thirty or forty codes that generate the bulk of the global sales. Another approach is to prioritize the products based on the level of reference risk that is present in each product. For example, you may find a small subset of product codes represent the bulk of the sales to global customers. In this case, it may make sense to focus on just those product codes first.

If, after completing the analysis and answering the questions above, you believe there is a significant potential for price referencing, then you will need to take action. So what can be done? There are a number of actions the firm can take to mitigate the risk of price referencing or price arbitrage. Four potential strategies will be discussed: implementing price corridors, changing the offering, setting a uniform price, and not launching the product in low-priced markets.

Risk Management Strategies
Implement Price Corridors

One of the approaches many firms use to address price referencing or arbitrage risk is to implement a price corridor. A price corridor is simply a mechanism for managing prices across markets. The "corridor" is the allowable range of prices within a country or region (5).

Figure 11.3 is an example of a price corridor. Since each county or region in many businesses is charged with growing sales and profits, they are usually focused on optimizing business in their own markets. This means that in order to implement a coordinated approach to pricing across markets, the company has to put in place process and organization to create and manage the pricing corridor.

The top of the corridor is the global list price, and the bottom is the global floor price. Often, firms set the price corridor within a specific region as well as globally. The floor price represents the price that is not to be sold below. In constructing price corridors, the firm has to answer a number of questions:

- Should a price corridor be set for all products or just those at a higher risk of price referencing?
- What is the allowable difference in prices across markets?
- How should choices be made between high- and low-priced markets?

Figure 11.3 – Pricing Corridor

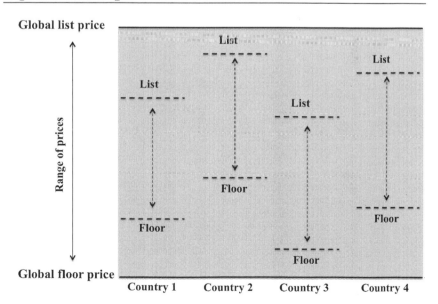

Constructing the price corridors requires analytics, but it also requires strategic thought and management judgment. For example, using Figure 11.3, assume countries 3 and 4 are bordering countries in Europe. Country 3 is a country with relatively low price levels driven by low reimbursement. Country 4 has relatively better reimbursement and higher price levels. In this case, the firm has to assess the potential financial impact to country 4 of selling at lower prices in country 3. The price differences have to be such that the firm can defend the prices to customers in the higher-priced markets. It will also have to assess the potential profit to parallel or gray traders of the price differentials. Often the impact of price referencing is not a one-time event but a permanent lowering of prices in the higher-priced markets.

Change the Offering

Sometimes firms choose to change the offering from one market to the next to avoid price referencing. This is popular in consumer markets where it is easy to change the physical product itself. In the medical technology industry, it is more difficult to do this given the regulatory approval process for products. Nevertheless, firms can look towards changing the offering in some way to differentiate it from one market to the next.

Table 11.2 – Offering Elements to Vary

Offering Elements	Description
Service level	Alter the level and type of service provided (e.g., 24x7 service vs. 8x5 service).
Shipping and delivery	Change the shipping and delivery terms.
Education/technical support	Adapt the amount or level of technical support and education provided.
Payment terms	Alter standard payment terms.
Financing	Change terms related to financing.
Order size/frequency	Adapt order size or frequency rules.

Consignment inventory	Decide to offer or not offer consignment or sequestered inventory.
Spare parts	Adapt or alter spare parts' pricing and terms.
Access to supplier capabilities	Limit or expand access to supplier capabilities to help customer grow.
Co-marketing	Select which customers or markets to offer or not offer co-promotional programs.
Co-development	Select when and with who to offer co-development arrangements.

If the firm cannot change the physical nature of the core product offering, there are other elements of the offering that can be adapted. Table 11.2 provides a summary of the potential elements of the offering that could be adapted.

The objective of changing the offering is to be able to defend the price against price referencing. For example, if a company sells a certain imaging technology in one market at a lower price than another market, then one of the ways to differentiate the offering and to defend the price differentials may be through altering one of the other offering variables, such as service levels. This would also presumably impact the cost to serve.

Set Uniform Price

Another way to minimize price reference risk is to set a uniform price and price structure across all markets. This could be the right strategy in some cases but may leave a lot of money on the table in other cases. In the case where there is one very large market and many other smaller markets, a firm may choose to set the price based on the value in the dominant market. This means that if there are wide differences in value and willingness to pay across markets, the firm could be missing profit opportunities in the smaller markets. The benefit of this type of approach is that the firm is assured to not suffer price referencing risk.

Don't Sell in Low-Price Markets

Another option firms have is to simply not sell the product in low-price markets. On the surface this seems like a reasonable strategy. It certainly has to be thought through very clearly. There are a couple of potential issues with this strategy. First, if you choose not to launch in the market, but a competitor will be launching soon, you run the risk of losing potential profits. Moreover, you have the risk of allowing your competitor to create a price referencing issues between the low-price and high-price market for their products, which in turn may impact your products.

So, part of the decision to not launch will be driven by what competitive alternatives exist and when those competitive alternatives might be available. Let's use an example. Suppose that you are launching a new technology and will be first to market. Also, assume that there are two competitors that will be launching a similar technology. One of the strategic issues you need to consider is whether to launch and at what price.

If the competitors are close behind you, and you choose not to launch in a given market, you allow your competitor to establish the market prices. This could be dangerous since the competitor may create a reference price risk that you had been trying to avoid. If, on the other hand, the competitors are far behind you, you have much more flexibility. In this case, you could choose to not launch in the market.

Conclusion

Global price difference is a real issue for medical technology firms. There are a number of external as well as internal drivers causing prices to vary across markets. Often, if left to itself, the price differences can be wide and cause lost profits and customer goodwill. The good news is that medical technology firms have a number of options to better manage price variation. These range from relatively simple to more complex solutions. The starting point is understanding the price differences. With an understanding of the differences, the firm then can assess the risks and take action.

NOTES

1. The idea for this chart was partially based on a different application of the concept in: Dolan, R. and Simon, H, (1996) Power Pricing. The Free Press. New York, NY.

2. See details in: Frost and Sullivan research reports http://www.frost.com/prod/servlet/report-brochure.pag?id=B673-01-00-00-00

3. Wall Street Journal; "New Stents, A Boon For Patients, May Affect Rising Health Costs", 12/26/02.

4. Cloft, H., et al. (2002) Assessment of the Interventional Neuroradiology Workforce in the United States: A Review of the Existing Data. AJNR 2002 23: 1700-1705

5. Simon, H. and Kucher, E. (1995) Pricing in the New Europe – A Time Bomb. Pricing Strategy and Practice 3:1 pp 4-13

INDEX

ABOUT THE COVER

The ubiquitous stethoscope represents one of the oldest types of medical devices invented that is still in use today. You are bound to see one at any visit to a doctor's office or hospital. It was invented in 1816 by a young French physician named René Théophile Hyacinthe Laennec. Dr. Laennec was trying to diagnose an obese patient who he suspected had heart disease. He rolled a sheaf of paper into a cylinder and, placing one end on the patient's chest, put his ear to the other end (you can read more at: Reiser, S., The Medical Influence of The Stethoscope. Scientific America. Feb., 1979). This is how a lot of the innovation in the medical technology industry happens. It is often clinicians, trying to solve real medical problems, who develop new tools and technologies with the help of medical technology companies.

The question is often how much is the technology worth? The cover is meant to reflect the value created by the medical technology, the exchange of money for the technology, and the diagnosing of value. These are all concepts and practices that are discussed in detail in this book.

I have to admit that the idea for the cover was not mine. I am a big believer in open-innovation. The basic premise of open-innovation is that there are a limited number of innovators in my network, but an unlimited number in the world. So, I turned to a service called crowdspring.com. This is a service that brings together creative designers from around the world with people seeking design help. The credit for the cover goes to adamesdesign.

ABOUT THE AUTHOR

Christopher Provines has over twenty-three years of global healthcare experience. He began his career in hospital finance. After graduate school, he joined Johnson and Johnson and later moved to Siemens Healthcare. His roles have included vice president-level positions at both companies. He has extensive global experience in a variety of functions, including strategic pricing, reimbursement, health outcomes, finance, procurement, commercial excellence, key account management, and business improvement. He is a world-leading thought leader in medical devices and diagnostics pricing. He is on the board of advisors for the Professional Pricing Society and is an award-winning adjunct professor at Rutgers University, where he teaches in the MBA program. Chris earned his MBA from Rutgers University.

Made in the USA
Lexington, KY
27 February 2013